Benjamin Cocar

EVANGELISM DISCIPLESHIP

The Great Commission of Making Disciples

EVANGELISM DISCIPLESHIP

The Great Commission of Making Disciples

Benjamin Cocar

Christian Publishing House
Cambridge, Ohio

Copyright © 2014 Christian Publishing House

All rights reserved. Except for brief quotations in articles, other publications, book reviews, and blogs, no part of this book may be reproduced in any manner without prior written permission from the publishers. For information, write,

support@christianpublishers.org

Unless otherwise stated, scripture quotations are from *The Holy Bible, English Standard Version®*, copyright © 2001 by Crossway Bibles, a publishing ministry of Good News Publishers. Used by permission. All rights reserved.

EVANGELISM DISCIPLESHIP The Great Commission of Making Disciples

Publishing by Christian Publishing House

ISBN-13: 978-0692359129

ISBN-10: 0692359125

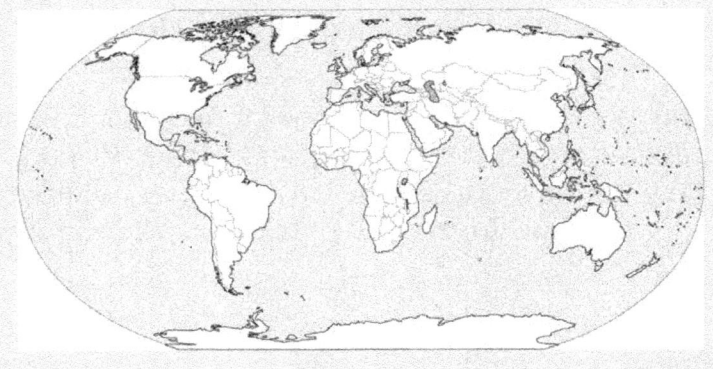

Matthew 28:18-20 Updated American Standard Bible (UASB)

[18] And Jesus came up and spoke to them, saying, "All authority has been given to me in heaven and on earth. [19] Go therefore and make disciples of all the nations, baptizing them in the name of the Father and the Son and the Holy Spirit, [20] teaching them to observe all that I commanded you; and lo, I am with you always, even to the end of the age."

PREFACE

Evangelism Discipleship is written with both the churchgoer and the seminary student in mind, as either can take advantage of its timely information. It is this author's hope that this publication can enable its readers to understand and appreciate what evangelism is, and who are obligated to carry it out.

Evangelism Discipleship will help its readers to ready themselves for what should be most important in his or her life. Our existence is the result of God creating us, so, to praise him and to understand fully the purpose of our lives will become all too clear before the close of this publication. Our heavenly Father deserves praise of the utmost excellence. (Rev. 4:11) What we learn herein will help us to accomplish this, enabling us to think in a logical, reasonable and unconfused manner, to act with wisdom, and communicate effectively the amazing truths from the inspired, fully inerrant Word of God.

PREFACE 6

INTRODUCTION 11
    Christian Ambassadors 18
    The Great Commission 18
    Give Us a Watchword 22
    Evangelize! Evangelize! 22

CHAPTER 1 What is Evangelism 23
    Who are Evangelizing? 24
    Our Message 25
    Forms of Evangelism 26
    First Good News 27
    Birth of Jesus Foretold 28
    Christ the Evangelist 30

CHAPTER 2 Who Can and Must Evangelize? 33
    All Christians are Expected to Carry Out the Work of An Evangelist 34
    First-Century Christians Evangelized 48

CHAPTER 3 Personal Evangelism 56
    Following the Example Set by Jesus 56
    Jesus as an Evangelist 59
    Jesus Begins His Ministry 60
    Saul Persecutes the Church 62

CHAPTER 4 Tools for and Forms of Evangelism ... 64

The Value of Knowledge and Wisdom 66
Bible Studies with Bible Students 69
Witnessing from House to House 71
Street Witnessing 79
Informal Witnessing 80
Telephone Witnessing 81
Returning to Evangelize Again 83
Witnessing to Strangers at Meetings 85
Witnessing by Our Conduct 85
Effective Use of Bible Tracts 85

CHAPTER 5 Other Methods of Evangelism 87
Mass Evangelism.. 87
Age-group Evangelism 88
Radio/television Evangelism...................................... 88
Bible Camp Evangelism... 89
Movies.. 89
Internet evangelism 90

CHAPTER 6 Difficulties in Evangelism....................91
Intimidation/fear 91
Unpreparedness of Mind and Heart 92
The Condition of the Unconverted 94

**CHAPTER 7 Evangelism Through the Local Church
.... 97**

The regular Meetings 97
Evangelistic Program 98
Excursion on Evangelism Program 98
Course Schedule 98
Door-to Door Evangelism 112
Vacation Bible Schools 113

CHAPTER 8 Everyday Informal Evangelism 115
What is Informal Evangelism? 116
The Evangelism Toolbox 117

CHAPTER 9 Common Excuses from Both Sides ... 120
Excuses of the Believers 120
Excuses of the Unbeliever 122
Evangelism and God's Sovereignty 124
Child Evangelism 127
How to Lead a Child to Christ 130
A Word of Caution 132
Evangelism Explosion 133

CHAPTER 10 The Importance of the Follow Up Ministry 141
Disciples are Made not Born 143
Spiritual Development 145
A Life of Discipline 148

APPENDIX A Teaching Our Children 151

Prayer for Spiritual Power 154
APPENDIX B The Field is the World 155
The Bloody City of Nineveh 156
APPENDIX C Evangelizing with a Spirit of Willingness 166
Warning the Wicked 167
APPENDIX D Using the Bible When We Evangelize 171
Something New to Share 173
APPENDIX E Bible Difficulties Explained 177
Inerrancy: Can the Bible Be trusted? 177
Inerrancy: Practical Principles to Overcoming Bible Difficulties 185
Inerrancy: Are There Contradictions? 195
Inerrancy: Are There Mistakes? 203
Inerrancy: Are There Scientific Errors? 208
Procedures for Handling Biblical Difficulties 240
Bibliography 242

INTRODUCTION

John 1:41 English Standard Version (ESV)

[41] He first found his own brother Simon and said to him, "We have found the Messiah" (which means Christ[1]).

"Word of mouth" is the use of oral communication to pass information from person to person--and we find good examples of it in the four Gospels as news about Jesus spread.

Scholars use the term "*oikos* evangelism" (*oikos* is Greek for household) to describe how people "gossiped the Gospel" from one household to another along natural lines of communication between family and friends.

While other forms of evangelism are good (rallies, literature, crusades), the most natural way to spread any kind of good news--especially good news about Jesus is, one person telling another. There is a level of credibility born out of personal experience and based on a history of trust, which makes personal evangelism effective. We can share the good news about Jesus nonverbally (the fruit of the Spirit: Galatians 5:22-23) and verbally. Ideally, when people come to respect the life we live before them, they become much more open to hearing the how and why.

All true theology has an evangelistic thrust, and all true evangelism is theology in action.—J. I. Packer

---

[1] In the NT, the word Messiah translates the Gk word *Christos* ("Anointed One"), except here and in Jn 4:25 where it translates *Messiah*.

Some people are afraid of the word evangelism. It gives Christians shame and guilt for not carrying out their responsibility, and it never produces a lot of enthusiasm among most Christians. It takes a book like "Radicals"[2] to move us to fulfill our obligation to Christ, but only for a short period, and then we switch back to our "normal" ways.

I learned personal evangelism in a communist country. It was very difficult to have a clear path to someone because you never knew if that person was an informer for the secret police. During my military service, the secret service of the army confiscated three Bibles from me, and wanted to court martial me because of Christian propaganda. When I left the service, they told me that I would be followed all my life. In ten years, I was in the United States of America.

I arrived in Detroit, MI in 1986, and I started sharing the Gospel with everyone I met.

After I completed my M.Div. at Detroit Baptist Theological Seminary, I was invited to teach evangelism at a local college. I asked the dean what he wanted me to do. He said only to share what I shared with the college in chapel, and it will be enough. For many years I taught evangelism, missions, and discipleship. In two or three colleges, I was asked to teach spiritual formation, which I did, but only in name. I taught discipleship, because the Bible does not have spiritual formation, only discipleship.

Our modern society did not invent evangelism. God started it. He sent us the "Good News," the Gospel when He sent us Jesus Christ, our Lord!

---

[2] **Radical: Taking Back Your Faith from the American Dream** by David Platt (May 4, 2010)

He was the Gospel, he proclaimed the Gospel, and charged his disciples to do the same. God has only One Son, and He made him a missionary for us!

Before Jesus left the earth, after his resurrection, he gave the disciples the command to make disciples.

1. <u>Matthew 28:19-20</u> The Great Commission//Going vs. walking

"Make disciples"

    a. baptizing--evangelism//missions

    b. teaching to obey all that Jesus said//discipleship

We cannot bring the whole world to Christ, but Christians have the obligation to take Christ to the whole world!

"Go into the entire world . . ." these were the words of our Risen Savior to his disciples. The whole world needs to hear the Good News, and the Christians must go and spread the good news.

The First Community Church of Jerusalem started as the result of the first evangelistic meeting held in Jerusalem in the Day of Pentecost. When the Holy Spirit descended upon the disciples, they started proclaiming the good news, the Gospel. They preached Jesus.

Persecution followed: They moved outside Jerusalem, and later we read in Acts 13:2 that the Holy Spirit called the first missionaries to go and spread the Gospel around the world. Then they did not have any missionary societies, or mission boards. Nevertheless, they knew to pray and fast. While they worshiped God, the Holy Spirit spoke, and immediately we read, "the two of them (Barnabas and Saul), were sent on their way by the Holy Spirit, and they went down to Seleucia, and sailed from there to Cyprus," Acts 13:4. From there world missions started. The mandate is the same for today's Christian, i.e., we are to "go into all the world!"[3] Barnabas and Saul responded to the call of the Holy Spirit and went, setting an example for all future generations of Christians. Jesus came into the world, and he knew how hostile this world is. Nevertheless, he came and died for it. Is it too much that he commands those whom he died for to go into all the world and tell the good news?

In 2 Corinthians 5:20 we read, "We are therefore Christ's ambassadors, as though God were making His appeal through us. We implore you on Christ's behalf: Be reconciled to God." We, the Christians are his ambassadors.

An ambassador in the Bible is an endorsed representative, who is sent out by one with a authority and power (e.g., a ruler), on special circumstances for a explicit reason. Generally, it would be an older, more mature man, who served in this capacity. Let us look at the Greek behind Ephesians 6:20, where Paul writes, "**I am an ambassador** [*presbeuo*] in chains that I may declare it boldly, as I ought to speak." At 2 Corinthians 5:20a, Paul writes, "Therefore, **we are ambassadors** [*presbeuomen*] **for Christ**, God making his appeal through us. At Luke 14:32 Jesus has been speaking of the cost of discipleship, when he speaks of a king that counts his cost of going to war with another nation, and

---

[3] Going into the world today need not mean that we pick up and travel to a foreign land. Rather, it simply means our community in which we live. Missions for centuries have carried out the aspect of going to the most distant part of the earth. Today, we need to do our evangelism right here in our own communities.

before going out to engage another king in battle, he "sends an **ambassador** [*presbeia*] and asks for terms of peace." These Greek words are related to *presbuteros*, which refers to an "older man," and "elder." Acts 11:30 says, "And they [disciples of Antioch] did so, sending [financial relief] to the **elders** [*presbuterous*] by the hand of Barnabas and Saul." At Revelation 4:4, it reads "Around the throne were twenty-four thrones, and seated on the thrones were twenty-four **elders** [*presbuterous*], clothed in white garments, with golden crowns on their heads.

Jesus Christ is the Son of God, who came as the Father's "apostle and high priest." (Heb. 3:1) It is he, who was sent by the Father to bring "brought life and immortality to light through the gospel."—2 Timothy 1:10

After Jesus ransom sacrificial death, resurrection, and ascension back to the Father in heaven, God in Christ appointed us as "ambassadors for Christ, God making his appeal through us." (2 Cor. 5:20) As ambassadors, we bear a message of reconciliation to God on behalf of Christ. We too are "an ambassador in chains," the chains of imperfection and human weakness, living in a world that is run by Satan the Devil, and his wicked henchmen, and we too need to 'declare it boldly, as we ought to speak." (Eph. 6:20) Our chains are an evident demonstration of the hostility that the world of humankind has toward us. These ones are alienated from God.—John 15:17-19

Whether a person accepts or rejects the ambassadors of God determines how God will receive him. Jesus himself stated, "Truly, truly, I say to you, whoever receives the one I send receives me, and whoever receives me receives the one who sent me." (John 20:30) As was briefly mentioned in the above, Jesus also used the illustration of a peace-promoting ambassador,

Luke 14:31-33 Lexham English Bible (LEB)

³¹ Or what king, going out to engage another king in battle, does not sit down first *and* deliberate whether he is able with ten thousand to oppose the one coming against him with twenty thousand. ³² But if not, *while the other* is still far away, he sends an ambassador **[*presbeia*]** *and* asks *for terms of* peace. ³³ In the *same* way, therefore, every *one* of you who does not renounce all his own possessions *cannot be* my disciple.

These passages were used to illustrate the disciple's need as an individual to sue for peach with the Father, where the disciple will give up his former life and ways, to follow in the footsteps of the Son, to attain a righteous standing before the Father, and have the hope of eternal life. On the other hand, he showed the foolishness of being connected with those sending ambassadors to speak contrary to the One on whom God places kingly power. (Lu 19:12-14, 27)

We have biblical examples of how ambassadors were used in the Hebrew Old Testament. On one occasion, to prevent war, we look to Jephthah, a judge in Israel. He sends out ambassadors to the king of the Ammonites, attempting to resolve a disagreement over territorial rights. The biblical account informs us "the king of the Ammonites did not listen to the words of Jephthah that he sent to him." (Judg. 11:28) Therefore, war was unavoidable, but God gave Jephthah the victory.

While the Israelites were wondering in the wilderness for forty years, they used ambassadors, in an attempt at gaining permission to pass through the Edomite territories. The ambassadors who were sent to the king of Edom said, "Please let us pass through your land. We will not pass through field or vineyard, or drink water from a well. We will go along the King's Highway. We will not turn aside to the right hand or to the left until we have passed through your territory." (Num. 20:17) The Edomites actually rejected this sound entreaty and declined to give authorization to the Israelites to pass. In fact, they even went a step further by sending out soldiers, to stop it. However, nothing in the account suggests that they harmed the ambassadors. Moses received the refusal from the ambassadors, so he took the Israelites around the land of Edom.

Ambassadors also had the task of taking challenges as well as pronouncements of war to the enemy. 2 Kings 14:8 says, "Then Amaziah sent messengers to Jehoash the son of Jehoahaz, son of Jehu, king of Israel, saying, "Come, let us look one another in the face." Rabshakeh was one of the ambassadors sent by King Sennacherib of Assyria, saying, "Say to Hezekiah, 'Thus says the great king, the king of Assyria: On what do you rest this trust of yours?'" Rabshakeh was declaring war on King Hezekiah, in behalf of the King of Assyria.

Regardless of the fact that Assyria, at that time, was the world power, and the most barbaric, feared empire, things did not go as planned. 2 Kings 19:35 says, "and that night the angel of the Lord went out and struck down 185,000 in the camp of the Assyrians. And when people arose early in the morning, behold, these were all dead bodies."

Christian Ambassadors

The Greek New Testament uses the term *ambassador* in a figurative sense, when it is applied to the disciples of Jesus Christ. Jesus was appoint by the Father as an ambassador of the kingdom, who was sent here to earth, to proclaim a message about the kingdom and its king. Therefore, Jesus' disciples were made ambassadors in his place here on earth after Jesus ascension, who were 'to proclaim in the gospel in the whole world as a testimony to all the nations, before the end would come.' (Matt. 24:14) Different from governmental ambassadors of Scripture and secular kingdoms, who were/are sent out by kings, the disciples of Jesus Christ are not being sent to the heads of kingdoms or governments. The Christian ambassadors were/are to carry the message of reconciliation, which is to be given to as a testimony to all people and all nations, so that they may be reconciled to the Father, through the Son Jesus Christ, by way of Christian ambassadors.

As the Christian ambassadors substituting for Christ make this plea to all individuals of this world, they need to respond by making peace with God through his Son, Jesus Christ; otherwise, they will be seeing the Son in a whole other capacity on the day of Armageddon. (Rev. 16:14, 16) In this way, Christ's born again, anointed disciples fulfill today the role of substitute ambassadors of the heavenly Father.

The Great Commission

The Church of the Risen Lord has a mission, and that mission is to take Jesus to the entire world. After two thousand years, there are many hundreds of millions without Christ. Worse still, there are hundreds of millions in denominations that do not reflect true Christianity, regardless of their claims. Why? There are many possible answers, but one is sure, the Church did not fulfill its mission. In today's society, if a company does not fulfill its mission, the owner will close it. There are no companies in America, which go without producing a product. The ones that are not working are declared bankrupt, and closed.

The Church of the Living God in its two thousand years of existence could not finish the task of taking the Gospel into the entire world, and Jesus did not declare it "bankrupt." In fact, there are no real true evangelism programs doing the work assigned by Jesus today. For 1,500 years, the Israelite nation was God's chosen people, who were so on again off again with their relationship with God, he closed them down. They were in and out of pagan worship, to the point of child sacrifice to the God of Molech. The only way to God after Jesus life and ministry was by way of Christianity. One either accepted Jesus Christ as the Son of God or not.—Matthew 21:43; 23:37-39

The last 2,000 years has seen the same from Christianity. In the first-century C.E., there was but one form of Christianity, the one Jesus started, and the apostles grew. By 200 C.E., there were twenty varieties of Christianity. By 400 C.E., there were eighty varieties of Christianity, and today, we have over 40,000 varieties. Those 2,000 years also saw some very serious on again off again worship as well, with a history far worse than that of the Israelites. Why has Jesus not closed out Christianity? Jesus asked a question that is related to this discussion,

Luke 18:8 English Standard Version (ESV)

⁸I tell you, he will give justice to them speedily. Nevertheless, when the Son of Man comes, will he find faith on earth?"

Jesus knows the future, and he foretold the great apostasy that overtook the church for a time. Moreover, the New Testament authors gave the same warnings. However,

Why did not close it down? Because He invested too much in it. He gave His own life for the Church, and He will bring the Church to the point of fulfilling its mission. When Jesus spoke for the first time about His Church, He said that the "gates of hell will not prevail against it," Matt. 16:18. Two thousand years of history proved that hell did not prevail against the Church. It slowed its movement, it hindered its advancement, but could not stop it. In all its history, the Church had people that paid attention to what Jesus said and went all over the world with the Good News. We know many, but we will know thousands only in eternity.

Among the last words of Jesus while He was on this earth were, "you will be my witnesses in Jerusalem, and in all Judea and Samaria, and to the ends of the earth," Acts 1:8. After those words, He went up to the Father. Now He is almost ready to come back to take up His Church. Is this generation ready to fulfill Jesus' words and proclaim the Good News, at home, in school, in our cities, country, and all over the world?

To fulfill the Great Commission we must evangelize.

Acts 2 tells about Peter's evangelistic sermon that presented Jesus Christ, God's Good News to this world, and the result was amazing, 3,000 people were saved, and baptized. The same chapter continues about the new converts spending time in "learning" what the apostles had to teach them. The apostles did not know much, only what Jesus told them!

Daily they studied the apostle's teachings, they prayed, they had fellowship, and celebrated the communion. They truly worshiped God!

2. <u>Mark 16:15-16</u> The Great Commission and its effects:

"Go into all the world and preach the Gospel," said Jesus, and those who will believe and will be baptized, will be saved, but those who refuse to believe will be lost. Sounds too simplistic . . . ? Yes, but this is God's way, and it is **the only way**!   Life and death are at stake, eternal life and eternal death!

3. <u>Acts 1:8</u> The Great Commission and its power

Remember, it is the Spirit of God, which does the work of bringing people to Jesus, we are the instruments that He uses, but the main part is His. Before the Day of Pentecost, the disciples were afraid to tell somebody about the Man they loved so much, (in fact they denied Him), but when the Holy Spirit came, they started to proclaim Jesus without any fear of men, Acts 2:14-41; 4:8-20. It is the Holy Spirit that came to present Jesus to this world, and to bring this world to Jesus. (See John 16:8) The Commander in Chief has given the order, the Captain of our salvation, the Lord Jesus, the only option we have is to evangelize. About 89% of Christians never pass an evangelistic tract in their lives . . . and that means that only **11%** of all Christians are really obeying Christ?

As a young Christian boy, in communist Romania, I had the privilege to read Oswald Smith's biography, and that burned in my heart to become an evangelist. I prayed and I cried many times to receive the fire that burned in Smith's heart to be also in my heart. God called me into the ministry, and for many decades, I preached and I called people to follow Christ.

Give Us a Watchword

Give us a watchword for the hour
A thrilling word, a word of pow'r
A battle cry, a flaming breath
That calls to conquest or to death
To heed the Master's high behest.
The call is given: Ye hosts, arise!
Our watchword is **evangelize!**
The glad evangel now proclaim
    Through all the earth, in Jesus's name;
This word is ringing through the skies:

Evangelize! Evangelize!

The dying men, a fallen race,
    Make known the gift of Gospel grace,
The world that now in darkness lies,
  Evangelize! Evangelize!
Oswald Smith

CHAPTER 1 What is Evangelism

Benjamin Cocar

What is Evangelism

In short, "pre-evangelism is *tilling the soil of people's minds and hearts to help them be more willing to listen to the truth*," while "evangelism is planting seeds of the Gospel." (Geisler and Geisler 2009, 22)

1 Corinthians 2:5 English Standard Version (ESV)

⁵ so that your faith might not rest in the wisdom of men but in the power of God.

The Greek verb for "bring good news," or "evangelize," is euaggelizomai (εὐαγγελιζομαι). The word *eu* (εὐ) meant in classical Greek, "well" in its kind, as opposed to the Greek word *kakos* (κακος) which meant "bad, evil, bad" in its kind, "ugly, hideous," and *aggellō* (ἀγγελλω) which meant, "to bear a message, bring tidings or news, proclaim." Thus, the verb means, "to bring a message of good news," and the noun, "good news." … The word *euaggelion* (εὐαγγελιον) was in just as common use in the first century as our words *good news*. "Have you any good news (euaggelion (εὐαγγελιον)) for me today?" must have been a common question. Our word *gospel* today has a definite religious connotation. In the ordinary conversation of the first century, it did not have such a meaning. However, it was taken over into the Cult of the Caesar where it acquired a religious significance. The Cult of the Caesar was the state religion of the Roman Empire, in which the emperor was worshipped as a god. When the announcement of the emperor's birthday was made, or the accession of a new Caesar proclaimed, the account of either event was designated by the word euaggelion (εὐαγγελιον). Thus, when the Bible writers were announcing the good news of salvation, they used the word *euaggelion* (εὐαγγελιον). (Wuest 1997, c1984, 3A_p.43)

Who are Evangelizing?

There are tens of thousands of different denominations, which call themselves Christian. Few if any of these denominations are carrying out a genuine evangelism program that is sharing biblical truth by going out into their community. Pre-evangelism and evangelism, i.e., proclaiming biblical truth, teaching and making disciples is the groundwork of true Christianity. It is the evidence that marks them as true, a sign that they are God's people, carrying out his will and purposes.

Some might ask, what about the missionaries? "In the unevangelized world, there are 20,500 full-time Christian workers and 10,200 foreign missionaries. In the evangelized non-Christian world, there are 1.31 million full-time Christian workers. In the Christian world, there are 306,000 foreign missionaries to other Christian lands. Also, 4.19 million full-time Christian workers (95%) work within the Christian world."[4] However, is this what Jesus and the New Testament writers had in mind, when they assigned every Christian to

---

[4] http://christianity.about.com/od/denominations/p/christiantoday.htm

evangelize, to carry out the great commission? (Matt. 28:19-20) No, this is not what Jesus or his New Testament authors meant. There is no denying the importance of missionaries in the spread of Christianity. However, the missionary has long displaced the Christian evangelist. It became convenient to train and send out (less than 1 tenth of 1 percent) 1.6 million volunteers throughout the world, while 2 billion so-called Christians (99.99 percent) stay home having little or no evangelism activity in their own community. First-century Christianity grew from 120 disciples in 33 A.D. to over 1 million by 120 A.D. They accomplished considerable growth with a handful of traveling missionaries, and almost all Christians evangelizing.

Our Message

What is our message, for those desiring to enter into the fray of becoming an evangelist for Christ? Jesus prophesied about his day up unto the time of his second coming, "This gospel [good news] of the kingdom shall be preached in the whole world as a testimony to all the nations, and then the end will come." Jesus commanded "Go therefore and make disciples of all nations ... teaching them. (Matt 28:19-20) Jesus later said that all future disciples from Pentecost to "the end" would "receive power when the Holy Spirit has come upon you, and you will be my witnesses in Jerusalem and in all Judea and Samaria, and **to the end of the earth**."—Acts 1:8

Thus, the foundation message of today's evangelist is the good news of the kingdom, under its ruler, Jesus Christ. (Isaiah 9:6-7) However, it is far more, as it would include the truths that Jesus spoke, the truths that the Old and New Testament author penned. It includes,

- sharing biblical truths,
- the preevangelism of "always being prepared to make a defense to anyone who asks you for a reason" (1 Pet 3:15),
- 'reasoning with them from the Scriptures, explaining and proving' (Ac 17:2-3),
- 'contending for the faith' (Jude 1:3),
- and 'saving others by snatching them out of the fire, helping those who have begun to doubt.' (Jude 1:22-23)

More could be said, but this is sufficient to make the point that much is expected and asked of the modern day Christian evangelist.

Forms of Evangelism

Some facets of evangelism are informal witnessing,[5] street witnessing, phone witnessing, house to house, and even the internet discussion boards. When one is actively involved in

---

[55] "This is sharing the good news with people as you come across them in the community: the store, doctor's office, public transportation, and so on. We are actively to seek out these ones in our everyday activities, such as a fellow employee, a fellow student at school, being served by a server at a restaurant, visiting a friend, and so on. All of these are acts of what is known as an informal evangelism. (John 4:7-15) These are unplanned but not unprepared occasions where we have an opportunity to share some form of biblical truths (Christian teachings) with another."—Edward Andrews.

the different facets of evangelism, it is an outward expression for their love for Almighty God and his neighbor. (Matt. 22:37-39) In addition, primarily, through evangelism God's supreme wisdom and infinite power are made known to our neighbors.—Acts 1:8; 4:33; Ephesians 3:10.

First Good News

God was the first evangelist, who brought humanity the good news. The Author of creation by way of Moses gave us the good news of the coming "seed." (Gen. 3:15) Then, the Father used the prophet Isaiah as an Old Testament evangelist, to tell us of the coming Messiah, i.e., Jesus Christ, further developing the good news of the seed, the one true evangelizer.

Isaiah 61:1 English Standard Version (ESV)

¹ The Spirit of the Lord God is upon me,
    because the Lord has anointed me
to bring good news to the poor;
    he has sent me to bind up the brokenhearted,
to proclaim liberty to the captives,
    and the opening of the prison to those who are bound

The Father has used others to inform us of this good news. He used might spirit creatures, angels, to share even more about this coming seed. Both the Hebrew word from the Old Testament (*malak*) and the Greek word from the New Testament (*angelos*), literally mean "messenger." In addition, "evangelist" comes from two Greek words, meaning "good" and "angel," i.e., "good messenger." For example, God used his angels, to 'preach the gospel beforehand to Abraham.' (Gal. 3:8; Gen. 22:15-18) The good news that Abraham received was that the "seed" was to come through his son. Through Abraham's seed God promised, "I will make of you a great nation, and I will bless you and make your name great, so that you will be a blessing." (Gen. 12:2-3) Almost 2,000 years later, the angel, Gabriel, served as God's evangelist, informing Zechariah, "I stand in the presence of God, and I was sent to speak to you and to bring you this good news." What was this good news? John the Baptist would be the greater Elijah, preparing the way for the greater Elisha, the seed of Abraham, Jesus Christ. (Lu 1:19) Then the angelic evangelist, Gabriel, was sent to Mary to build on this good news.

Birth of Jesus Foretold

Luke 1:26-38 English Standard Version (ESV)

[26] In the sixth month the angel Gabriel was sent from God to a city of Galilee named Nazareth, [27] to a virgin betrothed to a man whose name was Joseph, of the house of David. And the virgin's name was Mary. [28] And he came to her and said, "Greetings, O favored one, the Lord is with you!" [29] But she was greatly troubled at the saying, and tried to discern what sort of greeting this might be. [30] And the angel said to her, "Do not be afraid, Mary, for you have found favor with God. [31] And behold, you will conceive in your womb and bear a son, and you shall call his name Jesus. [32] He will be great and will be called the Son of the Most High. And the Lord God will give to him the throne of his father David, [33] and he will reign over the house of Jacob forever, and of his kingdom there will be no end."

[34] And Mary said to the angel, "How will this be, since I am a virgin?"

³⁵ And the angel answered her, "The Holy Spirit will come upon you, and the power of the Most High will overshadow you; therefore the child to be born will be called holy—the Son of God. ³⁶ And behold, your relative Elizabeth in her old age has also conceived a son, and this is the sixth month with her who was called barren. ³⁷ For nothing will be impossible with God." ³⁸ And Mary said, "Behold, I am the servant of the Lord; let it be to me according to your word." And the angel departed from her.

It was mere months later; the shepherds were also surprised by the visit of an angelic evangelist. "The angel said to them, 'Fear not, for behold, I bring you good news of great joy that will be for all the people. ¹¹ For unto you is born this day in the city of David a Savior, who is Christ the Lord. And this will be a sign for you: you will find a baby wrapped in swaddling cloths and lying in a manger." And suddenly there was with the angel a multitude of the heavenly host praising God and saying, 'Glory to God in the highest, and on earth peace among those with whom he is pleased!'" (Lu 2:8-14)

This would not be the end of the Almighty God use angel evangelists, as it continued on through the life and ministry of Jesus Christ 02 B.C.-33 A.D., up unto the death of the apostle John in 98 A.D. He used an angel evangelist to release the apostles from prison, commanding them to evangelize, "Go and stand in the temple and speak to the people all the words of this Life." (Ac 5:20) God then used his angelic messengers to aid human evangelist to carry out their evangelism program. This growth went from 120 on Pentecost, 33 A.D., to over one million disciples in the beginning of the second-century. (Ac 8:26; 10:3; 12:7-11) Finally, the apostle John, about 96 A.D., received a message from an angelic evangelist, where "he saw another angel flying directly overhead, with an eternal gospel to proclaim to those who dwell on earth, to every nation and tribe and language and people."—Revelation 1:10; 14:6.

Christ the Evangelist

Why was the early Christian church so courageous, active, and self-motivated in its evangelism? They had a foundational example like no other, the perfect evangelist, Jesus Christ. Jesus, with twelve apostle and hundreds of disciples, was a traveling evangelist for three and a half years, "to bring good news to the poor." (Isa. 61:1) At his ascension, Jesus left behind well trained evangelist to take the good news to the entire then known world.—Matthew 10:5-42; Luke 10:1-16.

Jesus was the most active evangelist this world has ever seen. He had inside understanding that not every human and angelic evangelist before him had, knowledge of his coming kingdom, which would bring true peace and security, replacing sickness, old age and death, with eternal life. He took in the spiritually sick condition of the people within the villages, towns and cities, as well as the countryside. Then he said to his disciples, "The harvest is plentiful, but the laborers are few; therefore pray earnestly to the Lord of the harvest to send out laborers into his harvest." (Matt. 9:37-38) Jesus was not just a man of words, but of action, as he commanded his apostle at once, "as you go, preach, saying, 'The kingdom of heaven is at hand.'" (Matt. 10:7, NASB) In all his divine wisdom, he did not campaign to be ruler, he did not set up some bureaucratic social program, nor did he start some religious activist movement. No, him simple objective was to "preach," i.e., Proclaim about the coming kingdom.

After handing out those assignments, Jesus have other evangelism instructions. After a return from a preaching campaign, Jesus said, with great joy, "I thank you, O Father, Lord of heaven and earth, that you have hidden these things from the wise and understanding, and have revealed them to babes. Yes, Father; for this was well-pleasing in your sight." (Lu 10:21, UASV) These so-called "babes" were not wise in the wisdom of the world. In addition, they were disciples, who began with no experience in communicating the truth of God to others, yet Christ taught these "babes" to be effective evangelists.

This preaching or proclaiming the truth of God to others was the groundwork that brought in over a million other disciples, from 120 to over a million in merely 80-years. All first-century Christians were evangelists. Yes, they obeyed the great commission, to "go therefore and make disciples of all nations, baptizing them ... teaching them." (Matt. 28:19-20) We have 120 who started by being given the power to miraculously speaking in other languages, 'telling others in their own tongues the mighty works of God." (Ac 2:4, 11) This miracle was not only used to make know the good news of God, but also to establish the new Christian church as displacing Judaism. Later that day, Peter made application of a prophecy from Joel,

Acts 2:17-18 (ESV)	**Joel 2:28-29** (ESV)
17 "'And in the last days it shall be, God declares, that I will pour out my Spirit on all flesh,	28 "And it shall come to pass afterward, that I will pour out my Spirit on all flesh;

and your sons and your daughters shall prophesy, 　and your young men shall see visions, 　and your old men shall dream dreams; ¹⁸ even on my male servants and female servants 　in those days I will pour out my Spirit, and they shall prophesy.	your sons and your daughters shall prophesy, 　your old men shall dream dreams, 　and your young men shall see visions. ²⁹ Even on the male and female servants 　in those days I will pour out my Spirit.

Prophecy (Heb., *nava*; Gr., *propheteuo*) has two meanings. The primary meaning is to proclaim truths about God's will and purposes to others. However, it is the second meaning, which gets the most press, foretelling the future. In the first-century A.D., all Christians were expected to evangelize (proclaim truths about God's will and purposes): men, women, even the youth. In those days, all were active in prophesying or proclaiming the good news of the kingdom. All first-century Christians were evangelizers.

CHAPTER 2 Who Can and Must Evangelize?

Edward D. Andrews

Romans 10:14 English Standard Version (ESV)

¹⁴ How then will they call on him in whom they have not believed? And how are they to believe in him of whom they have never heard? And how are they to hear without someone preaching?

Every Christian should realize that effective communication would be one of the determining factors in whether the unbeliever will accept the truth. Some may feel that the message will get through to the unbeliever, if he is receptive to the Good News regardless of communication skills. While that may be true on occasion, it is not the rule it is the exception. Moreover, it needs to be realized that our communicating skills are to be used to affect the hearts and minds of both the receptive and unreceptive. With the **unreceptive**, our skills must be stronger, as we are reasoning from the Scriptures, to overturn whatever has made this one unreceptive to the truth. It might be best if I were to put it this way, effective communication skills do not guarantee that one will accept the truth of God's Word, but a lack of communication skills means that it is far less likely that they will accept the truth of God's word.

Like a firefighter and a police officer, a Christian evangelist is on the job 24/7, as the opportunity to share a biblical message may occur at any time. Moreover, our conduct is always on display, and it is a form of witnessing to others. (1 Pet. 2:12) Whether we realize it or not we are always sending and receiving messages consciously and subconsciously with others by our tone, our demeanor, our body language, and so on. Again, our ability to communicate with clearness and precision, resolution and assurance is usually the difference between being successful and unsuccessful in our efforts to reach the hearts and minds of prospective (i.e., future) Christian disciples.

All Christians are Expected to Carry Out the Work of An Evangelist

Let us take a moment to listen to one of the world's leading authorities on Spiritual disciplines for our Christian life by Donald S. Whitney, who covers our obligation to evangelize very well,

> Most of those reading this book will not need convincing that evangelism is expected of every Christian. All Christians are not expected to use the same methods of evangelism, but all Christians are expected to evangelize.
>
> Before we go further, let's define our terms. What is evangelism? If we want to define it thoroughly, we could say that evangelism is to present Jesus Christ in the power of the Holy Spirit to sinful people, in order that they may come to put their trust in God through Him, to receive Him as their Savior, and serve Him as their King in the fellowship of His Church.[6] If we want to define it simply, we could say that New Testament evangelism is communicating the gospel. Anyone who faithfully

---

[6] See J. I. Packer, Evangelism and the Sovereignty of God (Downers Grove, IL: InterVarsity Press, 1979), pages 37-57.

relates the essential elements of God's salvation through Jesus Christ is evangelizing. This is true whether your words are spoken, written, or recorded, and whether they are delivered to one person or to a crowd.

Why is evangelism expected of us? The Lord Jesus Christ Himself has commanded us to witness. Consider His authority in the following:

"Therefore go and make disciples of all nations, baptizing them in the name of the Father and of the Son and of the Holy Spirit, and teaching them to obey everything I have commanded you. And surely I will be with you always, to the very end of the age" (Matt. 28: 19-20).

"He said to them, 'Go into all the world and preach the good news to all creation'" (Mark 16: 15).

"And repentance and forgiveness of sins will be preached in his name to all nations, beginning at Jerusalem" (Luke 24: 47).

"Again Jesus said, 'Peace be with you! As the Father has sent me, I am sending you'" (John 20: 21).

"But you will receive power when the Holy Spirit comes on you; and you will be my witnesses in Jerusalem, and in all Judea and Samaria, and to the ends of the earth" (Acts 1: 8).

These commands weren't given to the apostles only. For example, the apostles never came to this nation. For the command of Jesus to be fulfilled and for America to hear about Christ, the gospel had to come here by other Christians. And the apostles will never come to your home, your neighborhood, or to the place where you work. For the Great Commission to be fulfilled there, for Christ to have a witness in that "remote part" of the earth, a Christian like you must discipline yourself to do it.

Some Christians believe that evangelism is a gift and the responsibility of only those with that gift. They appeal to Ephesians 4:11 for support: "It was he who gave some to be apostles, some to be prophets, some to be evangelists, and some to be pastors and teachers." While it is true that God gifts some for ministry as evangelists, He calls all believers to be His witnesses and provides them with both the power to witness and a powerful message. Every evangelist is called to be a witness, but only a few witnesses are called to the vocational ministry of an evangelist. Just as each Christian, regardless of spiritual gift or ministry, is to love others, so each believer is to evangelize whether or not his or her gift is that of evangelist.

Think of our responsibility for personal evangelism from the perspective of 1 Peter 2:9: "But you are a chosen people, a royal priesthood, a holy nation, a people belonging to God." Many Christians who are familiar with this part of the verse don't have a clue how the rest of it goes. It goes on to say that these privileges are yours, Christian, "that you may declare the praises of him who called you out of darkness into his wonderful light." We normally think of this verse as establishing the doctrine of the priesthood of all believers. But it is equally appropriate to say that it also exhorts us to a kind of prophet hood of all believers. God expects each of us to "declare the praises" of Jesus Christ.[7]

While this author agrees with Whitney's every word in the above, I would emphasize that we are to evangelize, so as to make disciples, which is more involved that simply sharing the Gospel. Paul summarizes the most basic elements of the gospel message, that is, the death, burial, resurrection, and appearances of the resurrected Christ. (1 Cor. 18:1-8) Therefore, the Gospel explained in detail or simply stated as Paul has put it, will not be enough to convert many unbelievers to the faith. Therefore, it is best to understand our responsibility as evangelist, in the sense of being able to proclaim or explain our Christian teachings both offensively and defensively: to **(1)** defend God's Word, **(2)** defend the faith, **(3)** pull some who doubt back from the fire, and **(4)** most importantly, to help the lost find salvation.

All Christians are to be Evangelizers

We live in a world today where Genesis 6:5 and 8:21 is magnified a thousand fold.

Genesis 6:5 Updated American Standard Version (UASV)

⁵ Jehovah saw that the wickedness of man was great in the earth, and that every inclination of the thoughts of his heart was only evil continually.

---

[7] Whitney, Donald S. (2012-01-05). Spiritual Disciplines for the Christian Life with Bonus Content (Pilgrimage Growth Guide) (p. 100-101). Navpress.

Genesis 8:21 Updated American Standard Version (UASV)

²¹ And when Jehovah smelled the pleasing aroma, and Jehovah said in his heart, "I will never again curse the ground because of man, for the inclination of man's heart is evil from his youth. Neither will I ever again strike down every living thing as I have done.

Matthew 24:14 English Standard Version (ESV)

¹⁴ And this gospel [good news] of the kingdom will be proclaimed throughout the whole world as a testimony to all nations, and then the end will come.

With much of what people see today, one wonders what the Goods News could be.

Isaiah 52:7 English Standard Version (ESV)

⁷ How beautiful upon the mountains are the feet of him who brings good news, who publishes peace, who brings good news of happiness, who publishes salvation, who says to Zion, "Your God reigns."

Nahum 1:15 English Standard Version (ESV)

¹⁵ Behold, upon the mountains, the feet of him
  who brings good news,
  who publishes peace!
Keep your feasts, O Judah;
  fulfill your vows,
for never again shall the worthless pass through you;
  he is utterly cut off.

Romans 10:15 English Standard Version (ESV)

¹⁵ And how are they to preach unless they are sent? As it is written, "How beautiful are the feet of those who preach the good news!"⁸

Christianity today, has sadly, fallen away from the evangelism that they had been assigned, the preaching and teaching of the good news, the making of disciples. (Matt. 24:14; 28:19-20) The first-century Christians were very zealous when it came to sharing the good news and biblical truths with others. In fact, the new believers were taught the basics of the faith, before they were baptized. Once they were baptized they were immediately involved in spreading these same biblical truths to others. This is why just seventy years after the sacrificial death of Jesus Christ; there were more than a million Christians spread all throughout the then known world of the Roman Empire. Christians today, should have this same zeal, because Jesus gave only one command that was to be carried out after his departure, the making of disciples.

The good news is that this current evil age that we live in is not all that we have to look forward to, as all have the opportunity of gaining eternal life. Yes, the path of salvation is open to all. Therefore, Christians today should be in the work of being used by God to help as many as possible to find the path of salvation, before Christ's second coming.

John 3:16 English Standard Version (ESV)

¹⁶ "For God so loved the world, that he gave his only Son, that whoever believes in him should not perish but have eternal life.

---

⁸ Romans 10:15 : Cited from Isa. 52:7; [Nah. 1:15; Eph. 6:15]

John 3:36 English Standard Version (ESV)

³⁶ Whoever believes in the Son has eternal life; whoever does not obey the Son shall not see life, but the wrath of God remains on him.

Revelation 21:3-4 English Standard Version (ESV)

³ And I heard a loud voice from the throne saying, "Behold, the dwelling place of God is with man. He will dwell with them, and they will be his people, and God himself will be with them as their God. ⁴ He will wipe away every tear from their eyes, and death shall be no more, neither shall there be mourning, nor crying, nor pain anymore, for the former things have passed away."

Jesus Set the Example

Christians today should be seeking to walk in the steps of their exemplar, Jesus Christ. Yes, we have been called, so that we might follow in Jesus' steps.

1 Peter 2:21 English Standard Version (ESV)

²¹ For to this you have been called, because Christ also suffered for you, leaving you an example, so that you might follow in his steps.

Luke 4:17-21 English Standard Version (ESV)

¹⁷ And the scroll of the prophet Isaiah was given to him. He unrolled the scroll and found the place where it was written,

¹⁸ "The Spirit of the Lord is upon me,
   because he has anointed me
   to proclaim good news to the poor.
He has sent me **to proclaim liberty** to the captives

and recovering of sight to the blind,
to set at liberty those who are oppressed,
¹⁹ to proclaim the year of the Lord's favor."

²⁰ And he rolled up the scroll and gave it back to the attendant and sat down. And the eyes of all in the synagogue were fixed on him. ²¹ And he began to say to them, "Today this Scripture has been fulfilled in your hearing."

A survey of the Gospels indicates that Jesus' publishing program—via his traveling throughout Galilee and Judea and proclaiming the good news of the kingdom—was extensive and effective. Thousands and thousands of people heard the word from Jesus himself. In ancient times, the method of oral publication was far more effective than written publication. Books were expensive to make, and many people did not read. Most relied on oral proclamation and aural reception to receive messages. Indeed, most education was based upon oral delivery and aural reception/memorization to transmit texts. Thus, Jesus taught his disciples orally, and they committed his teachings to memory. When it came time, several years later, for the disciples to put these teachings into writing, they were aided by the Holy Spirit, who would remind the disciples of all that Jesus had taught them (John 14:26). Jesus' disciples, commissioned by him, continued the same publishing work after Jesus' death and resurrection. This publishing is known as the *kerygma* (Greek for "proclamation"). The word *kerygma* is taken straight from a well-known practice in ancient times. A king publicized his decrees throughout his empire by means of a *kerux* (a town crier or herald). This person, who often served as a close confidant of the king, would travel throughout the realm, announcing to the people whatever the king wished to make known. In English, we known him as a herald. Each New Testament disciple considered himself or herself to be like the *kerux*—a herald and publisher of the Good News.[9]

Yes, Jesus was an evangelizer, and he trained hundreds of evangelizers throughout his three and half years of ministry. "He went throughout all Galilee, teaching in their synagogues and proclaiming the gospel of the kingdom." (Matthew 4:23) Then he said to his disciples, "The harvest is plentiful, but the laborers are few; 38 therefore pray earnestly to the Lord of the harvest to send out laborers into his harvest." (Matt. 9:37-38) The apostles set up Christian congregations, with every Christian following the footsteps of Christ, to be an evangelizer.

While there is nothing, wrong with helping our neighbor deal with the social ills of the world, or taking some time to support a political candidate that we hope will implement laws that will allow for the greater work of evangelizing. Yes, Christianity has become a social institution, working night and day to save the world of humankind that is alienated from God, which has diverted them from the lifesaving work of being an evangelist. In the days of the Cold War between the United State and the former Soviet Union, a citizen of the United States would consider it treason if another citizen spent time promoting communism from the former Soviet

---

[9] Philip Comfort, *Encountering the Manuscripts: An Introduction to New Testament Paleography & Textual Criticism* (Nashville, TN: Broadman & Holman, 2005), 2.

Bloc. While we are citizens of this world, and of the country that we live in, our true Kingdom is the Kingdom of God in the person of Jesus Christ. Below we will quote the *Holman Illustrate Bible Dictionary* at length, to understand and appreciate what the Kingdom of God is.

The Kingdom of God

In the NT the fullest revelation of God's divine rule is in the person of Jesus Christ. His birth was heralded as the birth of a king (Luke 1:32–33). The ministry of John the Baptist prepared for the coming of God's kingdom (Matt. 3:2). The crucifixion was perceived as the death of a king (Mark 15:26–32).

Jesus preached that God's kingdom was at hand (Matt. 11:12). His miracles, preaching, forgiving sins, and resurrection are an in-breaking of God's sovereign rule in this dark, evil age.

God's kingdom was manifested in the church. Jesus commissioned the making of disciples on the basis of His kingly authority (Matt. 28:18–20). Peter's sermon at Pentecost underscored that a descendent of David would occupy David's throne forever, a promise fulfilled in the resurrection of Christ (Acts 2:30–32). Believers are transferred from the dominion of darkness into the kingdom of the Son of God (Col. 1:13).

God's kingdom may be understood in terms of "reign" or "realm." Reign conveys the fact that God exerts His divine authority over His subjects/kingdom. Realm suggests location, and God's realm is universal. God's reign extends over all things. He is universally sovereign over the nations, humankind, the angels, the dominion of darkness and its inhabitants, and even the cosmos, individual believers, and the church.

In the OT the kingdom of God encompasses the past, present, and future. The kingdom of God had implications in the theocratic state. The kingdom of God is "already" present but "not yet" fully completed, both a present and future reality. The kingdom was inaugurated in the incarnation, life, ministry, death, and resurrection of Jesus. God's kingdom blessings are in some measure possessed now. People presently find and enter God's kingdom. God is now manifesting His authoritative rule in the lives of His people. God's kingdom, however, awaits its complete realization. His people still endure sufferings and tribulations. When fully consummated, hardships will cease. Kingdom citizens currently dwell alongside inhabitants of the kingdom of darkness. God will eventually dispel all darkness. The final inheritance of the citizens of God's kingdom is yet to be fully realized. The resurrection body for life in the eschatological kingdom is a blessing awaiting culmination.

God's kingdom is soteriological in nature, expressed in the redemption of fallen persons. The reign of Christ instituted the destruction of all evil powers hostile to the will of God. Satan, the "god of this age," along with his demonic horde, seeks to hold the hearts of people captive in darkness. Christ has defeated Satan and the powers of darkness and delivers believers. Although Satan still is active in this present darkness, his ultimate conquest and destruction are assured through Christ's sacrificial death and resurrection. Sinners enter Christ's kingdom through regeneration.

Many of Jesus' parables emphasize the mysterious nature of God's kingdom. For example, an insignificant mustard seed will grow a tree, as God's kingdom will grow far beyond its inception (Matt. 13:31–32). The kingdom of God is like seed scattered on the ground. Some seed will fall on good soil, take root, and grow. Other seed, however, will fall on hard, rocky ground and will not grow. Likewise, the kingdom will take root in the hearts of some but will be rejected and unfruitful in others (Matt. 13:3–8). As wheat and tares grow side by side, indistinguishable from each other, so also the sons of the kingdom of God and the sons of the kingdom of darkness grow together in the world until ultimately separated by God (Matt. 13:24–30, 36–43).

Although closely related, the kingdom and the church are distinct. George Eldon Ladd identified four elements in the relationship of the kingdom of God to the church. The kingdom of God creates the church. God's redemptive rule is manifested over and through the church. The church is a "custodian" of the kingdom. The church also witnesses to God's divine rule.

The kingdom of God is the work of God, not produced by human ingenuity. God brought it into the world through Jesus Christ, and it presently works through the church. The church preaches the kingdom of God and anticipates the eventual consummation.[10]

The last sentence of our quote says in part, "the church preaches the kingdom of God." This has not been the case for almost 2,000 years. Today, the church preaches from the pulpit to those that are already Christian, as well as those, who happen into the church.

Romans 10:13-17 English Standard Version (ESV)

[13] For "everyone who calls on [through worship and prayer] the name of the Lord will be saved."

[14] How then will they call on him in whom they have not believed? And how are they to believe in him of whom they have never heard? And **how are they to hear without someone preaching**? [15] And how are they to preach unless **they are sent**? As it is written, "How beautiful are **the feet of those who preach** the good news!" [16] But they have not all obeyed the gospel. For Isaiah says, "Lord, who has believed what he has heard from us?" [17] So **faith comes from hearing**, and **hearing through the word of Christ**.

10:14b. Faith requires hearing. **And how can they believe in the one of whom they have not heard?** More than anything else, this question is the crux of all missiological activity since the first century. God has ordained that people must hear (or read, or otherwise understand the content of) the word of God in order to be saved. One who knows the

---

[10] Stan Norman with Gentry Peter, "Kingdom of God," ed. Chad Brand, *Holman Illustrated Bible Dictionary* (Nashville, TN: Holman Bible Publishers, 2003), 988–989.

gospel must communicate it to one who does not know it.[11]

Yes, missionaries have been sent out throughout the last few centuries, but this is not the first-century way, it is the way of the last few centuries. However, over the last few decades, many trained in missions have come to realize the error of their ways. They have tried to grow the church by going outside of their community, to grow it back to their community. This was mistake number one. The other alternative was to grow from your community out to the rest of the world. Their second mistake was to use just a select few (missionaries), believing they were going to get the Great Commission accomplished. Of late, we hear much about having missionary churches that evangelize their own community, with their own members. While this belief is best and correct, I am unaware of any that are doing it as it should be done, and most are not doing it at all.

10:14c. Hearing requires preaching. **And how can they hear without someone preaching to them?** Since no other media except the human voice was of practical value in spreading the gospel in the first century, **preaching** is Paul's method of choice. And yet, in the media-rich day in which we minister, has anything replaced preaching as the most effective way to communicate the gospel? We thank God for the printed page, and even for cutting-edge presentations of the gospel circling the globe on the internet. But it is still the human voice that cracks

---

[11] Kenneth Boa and William Kruidenier, *Romans*, vol. 6, Holman New Testament Commentary (Nashville, TN: Broadman & Holman Publishers, 2000), 314.

with passion, the human eye that wells with tears of gratitude, and the human frame that shuffles to the podium, bent from a lifetime of service to the gospel, which reaches the needy human heart most readily. Hearing may not *require* **preaching** in person today, but it always benefits from it.[12]

I agree with the Holman commentary that modern technology is great, but there is but one-way to reach "the whole world as a testimony to all nations" (Matt. 24:14). Yes, it is the human voice, but not as the Holman Commentary suggests with one man walking to a podium to preach, but for hundreds of millions to take to their communities, trained to preach (herald, proclaim) the message, and to teach what they had been taught "to one who does not know it."

First-Century Christians Evangelized

> [Jesus] reminded them in John 20:20 of his crucifixion: "He showed them his hands and side. The disciples were overjoyed when they saw the Lord." Then he reminded them again about his peace in verse 21. Jesus said, "Peace be with you!" Jesus proclaimed peace, reminded them of his crucifixion, pronounced peace again, and then told them, "As the Father has sent me, I am sending you" (John 20: 21). With that one command, Jesus announced two thousand years of direction for the church, still in effect for the churches of today, even your church. He proclaimed that we are sent. The church is, and you are individually, God's missionary to the world.

---

[12] Ibid., 314.

Your church is God's instrument to reach the world, and it includes reaching your community. We are sent on mission by God. We are to be a missions-centered church by calling, nature, and choice. We are called to be on mission in our community. We have been sent to be on mission in our context, and we must accept that call, that directive to be on mission where God has placed us, not five, not fifty, not five hundred years ago and not thirty miles away, not three hundred miles away, not three thousand miles away. We are exhorted to be on mission where God has placed us now, and our job is to [evangelize] wherever we are.[13]

Yes, the Great Commission was an assignment given to all Christians, which starts right in your own backyard. You can effectively evangelize the world, if you do it one community at a time, starting with your community.

Matthew 28:19-20 English Standard Version (ESV)

[19] Go therefore and make disciples of **all nations**, ... teaching them ... I am with you always, to the end of the age."

In the Greek, the words for "all nations" are *panta ta ethnē*. We get our English word ethnic from the Greek word *ethnē*. When we hear (or read) Jesus' command to "go to all nations," we think countries. But when Jesus spoke those words, there were no countries as we understand them today. The

---

[13] Putman, David; Ed Stetzer (2006-05-01). Breaking the Missional Code: Your Church Can Become a Missionary in Your Community (pp. 30-31). B&H Publishing. Kindle Edition.

nation-state is an invention of the modern era. In Jesus' day there were groups of people, and there were empires. Jesus' instructions mean that we must go to all the people groups in the world. The Jewish disciples of that day knew that Jesus was speaking about the Gentiles. The gospel was to go beyond the Jewish nation. But they also thought of Phoenicians, Macedonians, Greeks, Romans, and others Jesus did not use the word for empires like the Roman Empire, the Persian, or the Greek. Jesus used the word for peoples, and the Jews knew this meant all the different kinds of Gentiles. It meant to go to all the different kinds of people that existed. This is still God's plan today. In today's world, we have to remember that we are still sent ... to all different kinds of peoples. The word peoples represents every ethno-linguistic people group around the world, all the different ethnicities present in our cities, and even the different generations that live in our communities.[14]

Who all were involved in the evangelism work of the first-century? The evidence is all too clear that, all Christians were evangelizing their communities, with a select few, taking the message everywhere.

---

[14] Putman, David; Ed Stetzer (2006-05-01). Breaking the Missional Code: Your Church Can Become a Missionary in Your Community (p. 34). B&H Publishing. Kindle Edition

Acts 1:14 English Standard Version (ESV)

¹⁴ All these with one accord were devoting themselves to prayer, together with the women and Mary the mother of Jesus, and his brothers.

Acts 2:1, 4 English Standard Version (ESV)

¹ When the day of Pentecost arrived, they were all together in one place. ⁴ And they were all [men and women] filled with the Holy Spirit and began to speak in other tongues as the Spirit gave them utterance.

Acts 2:17 English Standard Version (ESV)

¹⁷ "'And in the last days it shall be, God declares, that I will pour out my Spirit on all flesh, and your **sons** and your **daughters** shall prophesy,*
    and your young men shall see visions,
    and your old men shall dream dreams; (See Joel 2:28-29)

* The Greek behind the word "prophecy" here does not carry the meaning of "prediction," or "foretelling," (Gr., *propheteuo*), but literally means "a speaker out [Gr., pro, "before" or "in front of," and *phemi*, "say"]" and thus describes a proclaimer, one who proclaims messages of God. That is, namely **"to proclaim an inspired revelation, *prophesy* ... Acts 2:17f; John 3:1; 19:6; 21:9; 1 Cor, 11:4f ...; 13:9; 14:1, 3–5, 24, 31, 39; Rev. 11:3** ...[15]

---

[15] William Arndt, Frederick W. Danker, and Walter Bauer, *A Greek-English Lexicon of the New Testament and Other Early Christian Literature* (Chicago: University of Chicago Press, 2000), 890.

Matthew 24:14 English Standard Version (ESV)

¹⁴ And this gospel of the kingdom will be **proclaimed throughout the whole world** as a testimony to all nations, and then the end will come.

Acts 1:8 English Standard Version (ESV)

⁸ But you will receive power when the Holy Spirit has come upon you, and you will be my witnesses **in Jerusalem** and **in all Judea** and **Samaria**, and **to the end of the earth**."

The prophecy of Jesus that the Good News would be **"proclaimed throughout the [then known] whole world** to all the nations [peoples], and then the end will come," was applicable to them, and was carried out. The "nations" (Gr., *ethnē*), means the same as it does at Matthew 28:19, where we are commanded to "make disciples of **all nations.**" The first-century Christians made disciples of **all nations** (the peoples), in all of **the then known world**,[16] before **the end came** for the natural nation of Israel, as the Romans destroyed Jerusalem in 70 C.E.,[17] killing over a million Jews, and taking hundreds of thousands captive. The apostle Paul wrote the Christians in Colossae about ten years earlier, 60 C.E, commenting on the spread of Christianity

---

[16] Christianity had spread from Jerusalem to Rome, Macedonia, Greece, Asia, Bithynia, Pontus, Galatia, Cappadocia, Pamphylia, Syria, Cyprus, Crete, Babylon, Persian Gulf, Spain, Italy, Malta, Illyricum, Media, Parthia, Elam Arabia, Cyrene, Libya, Egypt, and Ethiopia.

[17] Edward Andrews uses C.E., while Cocar uses A.D. Dates of events before the Common Era (Also known as AD) are marked by the abbreviation B.C.E. Dates of events during the Common Era are marked by the abbreviation C.E.

Colossians 1:23 English Standard Version (ESV)

²³ if indeed you continue in the faith, stable and steadfast, not shifting from the hope of the gospel that you heard, **which has been proclaimed in all creation under heaven**, and of which I, Paul, became a minister.

First-Century Christian Worship and the Truth

The early Christians met in congregations, which for many of them, were private homes, to take in the truth. (Rom. 16:3-5) The book of Hebrews tells us some of what took place at these meetings. They were there, in part, to "consider how to stir up one another to love and good works, not neglecting to meet together, as is the habit of some, but encouraging one another, and all the more as you see the Day drawing near." (Heb. 10:24-25) Tertullian of the late second, early third century (c.155–after 220 C.E.), wrote, "We meet to read the books of God … In any case, with those holy words we feed our faith, we lift up our hope, we confirm our confidence."[18] In order to become a Christian, certain requirements had to be met, as we can see from the *Zondervan Handbook to the History of Christianity*,

> As before, people who converted to Christianity were baptized. First, however, the new believer would be properly instructed in the beliefs and practices of Christianity. These 'beginner' Christians were the 'catechumens' (from the Greek meaning 'oral handing down', that is, teaching by word of mouth) and the way in which they were instructed developed as time went on. In the First apology,

---

[18] Thomas C. Oden, Ministry Through Word and Sacrament, Classic Pastoral Care, 59 (New York: Crossroad, 1989).

published in the middle of the second century, the Christian writer Justin Martyr (c. 100-165) gives us a valuable insight into how people were admitted into the church in Rome:[19]

> As many as are persuaded and believe that what we teach and say is true, and undertake to be able to live accordingly, are instructed to pray and to entreat God with fasting, for the remission of their sins that are past, we praying and fasting with them. Then they are brought by us where there is water, and are regenerated in the same manner in which we were ourselves regenerated. For, in the name of God, the Father and Lord of the universe, and of our Saviour Jesus Christ, and of the Holy Spirit, they then receive the washing with water.[20]

Thus, there were clear requirements before someone could be baptized: education of basic doctrinal beliefs, praying, fasting, and a commitment to live a moral life and an understanding of Christian beliefs. These new believers were discovered by taking the message into the community. Then, they were taught to become a disciple of Jesus Christ. They were then organized into Christian congregations. These same disciples (learners) were trained to make more disciples in the same way, preaching the Good News, and sharing the basic doctrinal beliefs.

---

[19] Jonathan Hill, *Zondervan Handbook to the History of Christianity*, 46 (Grand Rapids: Zondervan, 2006).

[20] Justin Martyr, "The First Apology of Justin", in The Ante-Nicene Fathers, Volume I: The Apostolic Fathers With Justin Martyr and Irenaeus, ed. Alexander Roberts, James Donaldson and A. Cleveland Coxe, 183 (Buffalo, NY: Christian Literature Company, 1885).

Acts 5:42 English Standard Version (ESV)

⁴² And every day, in the temple and from house to house, they did not cease teaching and preaching that the Christ is Jesus.

Acts 14:21-23 English Standard Version (ESV)

²¹ When they had preached the gospel to that city and had made many disciples, they returned to Lystra and to Iconium and to Antioch, ²² strengthening the souls of the disciples, encouraging them to continue in the faith, and saying that through many tribulations we must enter the kingdom of God. ²³ And when they had appointed elders for them in every church, with prayer and fasting they committed them to the Lord in whom they had believed.

Acts 20:20 English Standard Version (ESV)

²⁰ how I did not shrink from declaring to you anything that was profitable, and teaching you in public and from house to house,

While it is true that some are more gifted in the area communicating with others, no one should attempt to sidestep their obligation as an evangelist, who is responsible for carrying out the Great Commission of proclaiming the Good News, teaching, and making disciples. (Matt. 28:19-20) Some will make the argument that the Great Commission, and being an evangelist is a gift of the spirit, and only those called are obligated to do this work. This is not true, and is either a misunderstanding of Scripture, or one who is seeking to dodge the responsibility.

CHAPTER 3 Personal Evangelism

Benjamin Cocar

Jesus Christ, the Lord spoke to the multitudes, but occasionally he preferred to talk to one person only. In John chapters 3 and 4, we find two of the occasions.

Following the Example Set by Jesus

In John 3 a man, a teacher of the law came to see Jesus by night. Jesus took time to explain to him the new birth theology, and lead Nicodemus to believe in Christ.

1. Jesus was available
2. Jesus was patient
3. Jesus was persistent
4. Jesus was clear in His presentation

Later in Gospel, we read that Nicodemus had the courage to go to Pilate and ask permission to take Jesus' body and bury it, John 19:39.

In John 4, Jesus met a woman of bad reputation and **in simple words**; he led her to the knowledge of the Messiah.

1. Jesus **looked for this opportunity** ... he could follow the "detour" road of the Jews, but he did not. He went through Samaria because of this "divine appointment."

2. Jesus used a **very normal, non-threatening approach** to evangelism, "give me to drink."

3. He **listened to her** theological explanations about places and styles of worship. How often we do not listen. We

have the right message and we keep pressing it ...   Jesus was a listener!

4. Jesus confronted her **at the right point**, "bring your husband."

As a result, the woman was saved, and she went to tell others about the man who saved her, "told her all about herself."

Jesus was not the only one who did **personal evangelism**. His disciples did personal evangelism as well.

Philip had to leave a very successful (and effective) evangelistic ministry in Samaria, and went on a deserted road to witness to the Ethiopian eunuch, Acts 8:6-8, 26-39. Knowing why God did not find another man to send him instead of Philip is impossible, but this shows how important personal evangelism is.

Philip did not shout, "Hey man, are you saved?" No. He asked him if he understand God's Word, and he was **ready to listen** to what the eunuch had to say. He was **prepared** what **to answer**. He knew his lesson well (all the prophetic material about Jesus!). He **does not push** the man for a "decision, "but the man asked him. Philip followed his request and baptized the eunuch.

Peter had to go to the house of Cornelius, (Acts 10), and Paul preached the Gospel to the Philippian jailor, (Acts 16).

Personal evangelism is part of the great plan of bringing people to a personal relationship with Jesus Christ.

We can plan personal evangelism or we can do it completely unplanned, i.e., informal.

A. planned personal evangelism:

    1. individual planning (preparation for special situations)

    2. through the local church (churches plan and send individuals around the neighborhood)

B. unplanned personal evangelism (living daily the Christian witness!)

    1. the most common situations can be turned into excellent opportunities for sharing the Gospel

    2. The opportunities abound

        (1) We must recognize them

        (2) We must capture them

        (3) We must be ready

        (4) We must have our hearts prepared

        (5) We must know the simple plan of salvation:

            (a) Romans 3:23--All have sinned

            (b) Romans 6:23--The penalty for sin

            (c) Hebrews 9:27--Penalty must be paid

            (d) Romans 5:8--Penalty paid by Christ

            (e) Ephesians 2:8-9--Salvation a free gift

            (f) John 1:12--Must receive Christ

            (g) Revelation 3:20--Christ at the heart's door

            (h) 1 John 5:11-12--Assurance of salvation

        (6) We must be ethical, and use common sense

        (7) We must avoid embarrassment

(8) We must know when to desist/do not give up easily, we must know the difference

The advantages of personal evangelism:

1. All Christians can do personal evangelism

    a. not all of them can preach, teach or sing in a church but all can share the Gospel to a friend

    b. not everyone uses the same method, but the same message

    c. the results are not the same

2. Attention is given to the individual

    a. each of us is different

    b. conformity and distinction are part of our personalities

3. It enables one to deal with personal problems

4. It shows the strength and the weakness of the evangelist

Jesus as an Evangelist

Earlier we learned something that we may have never contemplated before. God use both angels and humans as evangelists, both in the Old and New Testament. Angels were sent to Abraham. Elijah and Elisha were two of the foremost evangelists of Israel. Before the arrival of the Son of God, he raised up John the Baptist as the greater Elijah (Mal. 4:4-6, AS), who announced the coming of the Messiah. We learned that an angelic evangelist appeared to both Zechariah, announcing that he would have a son, and that same angel appeared to Mary, informing her that she would be giving birth to the Son of God. This Son of God would group up to become the greatest evangelist this earth has ever known.

Jesus Begins His Ministry

For thirty years, Jesus was the son of a carpenter. In about 29 A.D., Jesus came to his hometown of his childhood.

Luke 4:14-22 English Standard Version (ESV)

14 And Jesus returned in the power of the Spirit to Galilee, and a report about him went out through all the surrounding country. 15 And he taught in their synagogues, being glorified by all.

16 And he came to Nazareth, where he had been brought up. And as was his custom, he went to the synagogue on the Sabbath day, and he stood up to read. 17 And the scroll of the prophet Isaiah was given to him. He unrolled the scroll and found the place where it was written,

18 "The Spirit of the Lord is upon me,
   because he has anointed me
   to proclaim good news to the poor.
He has sent me to proclaim liberty to the captives
   and recovering of sight to the blind,
   to set at liberty those who are oppressed,
19 to proclaim the year of the Lord's favor."

20 And he rolled up the scroll and gave it back to the attendant and sat down. And the eyes of all in the synagogue were fixed on him. 21 And he began to say to them, "Today this Scripture has been fulfilled in your hearing." 22 And all spoke well of him and marveled at the gracious words that were coming from his mouth. And they said, "Is not this Joseph's son?"

The good news was not well received in Jesus' hometown. The Nazarenes became upset at what Jesus preached. They even went so far as to try to take his life. (Lu 4:22-30) However, Jesus was not dissuaded from the commission to evangelize that he had received from the Father, moving on elsewhere, seeking out those who were receptive to the good news. Luke tells us, "Soon afterwards, He began going around from one city and village to another, proclaiming and preaching the kingdom of God. The twelve were with Him," (Luke 8:1, NASB; Mark 1:14-15) Yes, Jesus was an evangelist of God's kingdom. He sent for his disciples as evangelists, instructing them, "As you go, preach, saying, 'the kingdom of heaven is at hand.'"—Matthew 10:1-7.

Even death did not stop the evangelism work of Jesus. The Jewish religious leaders despised Jesus and the good news he brought. They falsely accused him of forbidding the paying of taxes and treasonously trying to make himself king, which would be in opposition to Tiberius Caesar. (John 19:12-16) After being beaten and executed, and raised on the third day, Jesus picked up his evangelism work for forty days, until his ascension. No fear, though, Jesus had promised, "I am with you always, even to the end of the age." (Matt. 28:20) Yes, Jesus continued to supervise the evangelism program from heaven, giving direction to his evangelists on earth. Even though the intensity of the enemies of the good news grew, Luke tells us "every day, in the temple and from house to house, they did not cease teaching and preaching that the Christ is Jesus."—Acts 5:42.

Many think of Peter, Paul, Barnabas, Silas, Philip, and others as the evangelists of the first-century A.D. However, this would be a mistaken view, as all Christians within all churches were evangelists, obligated to share the biblical truths will all, who would listen. Even the persecution that befell the early church from 36 A.D., up unto to 325 A.D., did not dissuade the everyday Christians from sharing the good news with others. In fact, the persecution Jews, pagan, and the Roman government, actually helped the growth of Christianity.

Saul Persecutes the Church

The Apostle Paul was known as Saul, before becoming a Christian. Saul studied under Gamaliel, the greatest Jewish scholar of that period. Saul was destined for greatness as a Pharisee, because of his renowned teacher and his level of education in Judaism.

Saul saw Christianity as an apostate religion, a break away from Judaism. For Saul, the true way to God had been through the Israelite nation, since the days of Abraham, their ancestor, some 2,060 years before the days of Saul. Yes, they awaited the Messiah, the seed of Abraham, but to Saul, Jesus Christ was the furthest thing from the long awaited anointed one. Why?

The messiah was to destroy all kingdoms and set up a throne that would never be brought to ruin; he was to usher in an era of real peace and security. Jesus did no such thing. In fact, Deuteronomy says anyone hung upon a tree, was cursed by God, and Jesus was hung upon a tree.

When the Jews stoning of Stephen evangelism was under fierce persecution it is written,

Acts 8:1, 2, 4, 5, 12 English Standard Version (ESV)

[1] And Saul approved of his execution.

And there arose on that day a great persecution against the church in Jerusalem, and they were all scattered throughout the regions of Judea and Samaria, except the apostles. ² Devout men buried Stephen and made great lamentation over him. ⁴ Now those who were scattered went about preaching the word. ⁵ Philip went down to the city of Samaria and proclaimed to them the Christ. ¹² But when they believed Philip as he preached good news about the kingdom of God and the name of Jesus Christ, they were baptized, both men and women.

Yes, Saul went on a mission of persecuting Christians, even supporting the stoning of Stephen. On the road to Damascus, he came face to face with the risen Lord, Jesus Christ. He was blinded and taken to Damascus, where Ananias was sent to minister to him.

Ananias showed Saul from the Scriptures that the Jewish expectations were misleading. Jesus was not to set up his kingdom on his first arrival because, at that time, he needed to offer himself as a ransom for many. It would be his second coming, in which he would set up the kingdom

Yes, Jesus was not cursed because he hung upon a tree, but rather he carried imperfect humanities curse. Once Saul had his face to face with the risen Lord and the exposition from the Hebrew Scriptures from Ananias, he could no longer deny the truth; Jesus Christ was the long awaited Messiah.

Saul started going by his Roman name Paul and became a Christian, giving his life for 30 years of torture, pain, suffering, sickness, stoning, beatings, shipwreck, and eventually martyrdom.

CHAPTER 4 Tools for and Forms of Evangelism

Edward D. Andrews

"Do the work of an evangelist," was the charge of Paul to young Timothy. (2 Tim 4:5) The work of an evangelist is to evangelize. The Bible does not tell us about Timothy's tools,[21] but we can read in the letters that Paul's books were in Timothy's care. More, we read how much Paul is writing about prayer. We can conclude that Timothy prayed and studied the Scriptures.

We have to begin with the same tools, reading, studying the Bible, and prayer.

The Bible: There is no better tool than God's Word. Know the Word of God. Be familiar with the Old Testament, but for evangelism, be an expert in the New Testament. Memorize as many verses as you can. Be always ready to quote as many verses as presenting the Gospel is necessary.

Prayer: Prayer must be a characteristic of every Christian. We pray to live our Christian lives. In witnessing, prayer is vital. It shows that we are aware that the Holy Spirit does the main part in evangelism. Pray before any occasions of planned personal evangelism, but be ready to pray even when unplanned situations occur. Entrust in prayer all the

---

[21] However, we do know that the second greatest evangelist of all times was the apostle Paul, only bested by Jesus Christ himself. Young Timothy spent 15-years as a traveling companion and coworker with Paul. Those who have more experience need to take younger less experienced ones under their supervision.

witnessing. Ask to Lord to continue all what you started. Remember, you plant the seed, others may come and water it, but the Lord helps it grow.

Keep it Simple: The apologist's words should always be seasoned with salt as we share the unadulterated truths of Scripture with gentleness and respect. Our example in helping the unbeliever to understand the Bible has been provided by Jesus Christ and his apostles. Whether dealing with Bible critics or answering questions from those truly interested ones, Jesus referred to the Scriptures and at time used appropriate illustrations, helping those with a receptive heart to accept the Word of God. The apostle Paul "reasoned with them from the Scriptures, explaining and proving" what was biblically true. (Ac 17:2-3)

Bible Knowledge: There is a great deal of irony in that the Scriptures are fill with verses that exhort, expound, implore, command, demand that the servant of God take in and have knowledge of the Word of God. However, many pastors and bible teachers say things like, "a relationship with God is not about head knowledge," or "it is not all about the head knowledge." Some say to those that have a deep understanding of God's Word, "oh that's head knowledge, and not heart knowledge."

Because the last generation of Christian leaders had worked so hard to downplay the need of taking in knowledge of God, it has gotten to the point that this generation does not believe that we need a deeper knowledge of God. They know nothing of apologetics, which is pre-evangelism. Biblical illiteracy has abounded and this has led to losing millions to the evangelism of atheism. That is right, you heard it correctly, atheists evangelize more than

Christians do, and they are usually better informed. Over the last 30-years, while Christianity has turned its back on the deeper things of God's Word, the new atheism has went on an evangelism campaign that includes witnessing to Christians, books, tracts, radio, television, internet, and so on. Do the following texts sound as though we are to abandon taking in knowledge?

The Value of Knowledge and Wisdom

Joshua 1:8 English Standard Version (ESV)

⁸ This Book of the Law shall not depart from your mouth, but you shall meditate on it day and night, so that you may be careful to do according to all that is written in it. For then you will make your way prosperous, and then you will have good success.

Deuteronomy 6:6-9 English Standard Version (ESV)

⁶ And these words that I command you today shall be on your heart. ⁷ You shall teach them diligently to your children, and shall talk of them when you sit in your house, and when you walk by the way, and when you lie down, and when you rise. ⁸ You shall bind them as a sign on your hand, and they shall be as frontlets between your eyes. ⁹ You shall write them on the doorposts of your house and on your gates.

Psalm 1:1-3 English Standard Version (ESV)

¹ Blessed is the man
   who walks not in the counsel of the wicked,
nor stands in the way of sinners,
   nor sits in the seat of scoffers;
² but his delight is in the law of the Lord,
   and on his law he meditates day and night.

³ He is like a tree
　　planted by streams of water
that yields its fruit in its season,
　　and its leaf does not wither.
In all that he does, he prospers.

Proverbs 2:1-6 English Standard Version (ESV)

¹ My son, if you receive my words
　　and treasure up my commandments with you,
² making your ear attentive to wisdom
　　and inclining your heart to understanding;
³ yes, if you call out for insight
　　and raise your voice for understanding,
⁴ if you seek it like silver
　　and search for it as for hidden treasures,
⁵ then you will understand the fear of the Lord
　　and find the knowledge of God.
⁶ For the Lord gives wisdom;
　　from his mouth come knowledge and understanding;

Hosea 4:6 English Standard Version (ESV)

⁶ My people are destroyed for lack of knowledge;
because you have rejected knowledge,
　　I reject you from being a priest to me.
And since you have forgotten the law of your God,
　　I also will forget your children.

John 17:3 English Standard Version (ESV)

³ And this is eternal life, that they know you the only true God, and Jesus Christ whom you have sent.

Philippians 1:9 English Standard Version (ESV)

⁹ And it is my prayer that your love may abound more and more, with knowledge and all discernment,

2 Peter 3:18 English Standard Version (ESV)

¹⁸ But grow in the grace and knowledge of our Lord and Savior Jesus Christ. To him be the glory both now and to the day of eternity. Amen.

When we think of the great apologists of today, name that come to mind are William Lane Craig, Ravi Zacharias, Norman L. Geisler, Josh McDowell, Sean McDowell, John Lennox, Frank Turek, Alex McFarland, and Lee Strobel, to mention just a few. Churches are seeking apologists such as these to speak at their churches to revitalize the need for a deeper understanding of God's Word. We now have a mad rush of Christian leaders trying to get the genie back in the bottle, i.e., head knowledge back in the minds of the Christians. We have hundreds of millions of Christians that are biblically illiterate, meaning that they are unable to teach the foundational doctrines, and they cannot defend the faith or the Bible.

We have already established that we (all Christians) are under obligation, commanded by Jesus Christ to proclaim, teach, and make disciples. How are we to teach another, if we have not first been taught ourselves? If we are to teach others, we must fully and clearly understand the subject ourselves. If we are to make it easy to understand, we have to have a deeper knowledge of God ourselves. When we truly understand a subject, we find it much easier to teach it to others, and defend its position.

Romans 10:14-15 English Standard Version (ESV)

¹⁴ How then will they call on him in whom they have not believed? And how are they to believe in him of whom they have never heard? And how are they to hear without someone preaching? ¹⁵ And how are they to preach unless they are sent? As it is written, "How beautiful are the feet of those who preach the good news!"

Below are several forms of evangelism by Edward D. Andrews,[22]

Bible Studies with Bible Students

Below we will discuss several different forms of evangelizing friends, family, and our local community. The goal of every witnessing opportunity is to start a one-on-one Bible study with the person, preferably in their home, once a week for an hour. All congregation members, who are active in the evangelism of their community, should be able to carry on a Bible study program with a new one. There should be a basic theology book, like Concise Bible Doctrines by Elmer Towns, which could be used as a study tool. You do not want people becoming a member of your congregation based on emotionalism. Rather, you want then joining because they are able to make an informed decision based on knowledge of the Scriptures.

These studies can be carried out in their home, or in your home, even in the congregation if it is open and available. It is a one-on-one study with you and him or her. Your

---

[22] Edward D. Andrews, THE EVANGELISM HANDBOOK: How All Christians Can Effectively Share God's Word in Their Community, 122-142 (Cambridge, OH: Christian Publishing House, 2013).

objective is to go through two books. The first book would be on doctrinal beliefs. The second book would be on the basics of how to interpret Scripture. This book highly recommends, *Basic Bible Interpretation* by Roy B. Zuck (Jan 1991).[23] Of course, you want to invite them to church, offering them transportation, if needed. Throughout this study process of several months, the objective is more involved than taking in knowledge (while this is important), but also includes helping them as they transition from the world, to the Christian faith, putting on that new Christ-like person. (Eph. 4:23-24; Col. 3:8-10) They should be treated as if they are your spiritual child. (1 Cor. 4:17)

If a congregation chooses to use Elmer Towns' book, *Concise Bible Doctrines*, it should be noted that this book does not have any study questions at the end of its short chapters. Therefore, the person in charge of the Evangelism program must study through the book himself first, making a study sheet as he goes. This study sheet would be used thereafter as people in the church study this book as well. Then, the study sheet would be given to the bible student of the congregation member, along with his or her copy of the book. It would be explained to the Bible student, that he or she is to prepare for the study beforehand, by going through the section the teacher assigns, reading, looking up the Scriptures, and underlining or highlighting the answers to the questions. When the study is conducted, the student should save any question they may have written down, until they have covered the assignment first.

---

[23] ISBN-13: 978-0781438773

Witnessing from House to House

Two groups are known the world over for this form of evangelism, Jehovah's Witnesses and Mormons. However, I have had a few Baptist pastors come to my door, which was a surprise. This form of evangelism should not be shied away from because one does not want to be affiliated with Witnesses and Mormons. The early Christians carried out a house-to-house evangelistic work (Luke 9:1-6; 10:1-7; Acts 5:42;[24] 20:20), and there has never proven to be a more foundational way of reaching your neighbor. This is a difficult work, as most people are not receptive to God's Word, seeing it as a book by man, foolish and outdated. Therefore, it takes a true love for God and neighbor to be out in our community repeatedly, year after year, engaged in a world that is uninterested, and in opposition to the work, which Jesus assigned.

2 Corinthians 2:14-17 English Standard Version (ESV)

14 But thanks be to God, who in Christ always leads us in triumphal procession, and through us spreads the fragrance of the knowledge of him everywhere. **15** For we are the aroma of Christ to God among those who are being saved and among those who are perishing, **16** to one a fragrance from death to death, to the other a fragrance from life to life. Who

---

[24] R. C. H. Lenski, in his work The Interpretation of The Acts of the Apostles, Minneapolis (1961), made the following comment on Ac 5:42: "Never for a moment did the apostles cease their blessed work. 'Every day' they continued, and this openly 'in the Temple' where the Sanhedrin and the Temple police could see and hear them, and, of course, also *kat oikon*, which is distributive, 'from house to house,' and not merely adverbial, 'at home.' "

is sufficient for these things? **17** For we are not, like so many, peddlers of God's word, but as men of sincerity, as commissioned by God, in the sight of God we speak in Christ.

Holman New Testament Commentary

2:14a. Paul had been disappointed in Troas and Macedonia, but through it all God had been good to him. He began this acknowledgment of divine goodness with thanksgiving: **But thanks be to God**.

2:14b–16a. Paul delighted in God's care for him. He expressed this joy with the metaphor of a victory parade. Paul was convinced that God **always leads** believers **in triumphal procession in Christ**. Paul drew upon the triumphal parades that were known throughout the Roman world. Prisoners of war were marched through the streets as fragrant perfumes filled the air. At the end of each parade, many prisoners were executed. For this reason, the smells of the parade were sweet to the victors, but they were the **smell of death** to the defeated.

Paul saw several similarities between these victory parades and his own ministry. (1) He and those with him were members of the victorious army led by **Christ**, as were the rest of the apostles. (2) Their gospel preaching spread **everywhere ... the knowledge** or acknowledgment **of God** as the victor. Similarly, Roman victory parades spread knowledge about victories and caused people to acknowledge the victors. (3) Paul said that he and the apostles were like the perfumes of the victory parades. They became **to** (the honor of) **God** like **the aroma of Christ**, or more specifically, like **the**

aroma accompanying Christ's victory. Both the victors of this spiritual gospel war (**those who are being saved**) and the defeated (**those who are perishing**) smelled their **aroma**. (4) This **aroma of Christ**, however, affected each group differently. To Christ's enemies, Paul and those with him were **the smell of death**, but to those following Christ they were **the fragrance of life**.

This metaphor contrasted Christian and non-Christian reactions to evangelists. To Christians, Paul and his company presented reminders of the wonders of salvation. For non-Christians, they raised the terror of divine judgment. No one could ignore them because their fragrance was spreading throughout the world.

2:16b. As Paul contemplated his analogy between Roman victory parades and his gospel ministry, he was overwhelmed. He exclaimed, **Who is equal to such a task?** The answer he implied was that no one was worthy of playing such an important role in human history and in the kingdom of God. It was astounding that God appointed humans to this role.

2:17. Paul wanted the Corinthians to know that he did not view his ministry as an ordinary job. He did not **peddle the word of God for profit**. He distinguished himself and those who worked with him from **so many** others who had reduced their ministries to mere occupations. Unlike the gospel peddlers, Paul and his company spoke **before God with sincerity**. Paul still lingered on the accusation of insincerity and duplicity he had addressed in the preceding section. He could not have been insincere because he looked upon his ministry so highly. Instead, he served as one **sent from God**, considering his task a sacred privilege. The fact that he did not accept payment for his preaching further demonstrated his sincerity.[25]

Zondervan Illustrated Bible Backgrounds Commentary

And through us spreads everywhere the fragrance of the knowledge of him (2:14). One of the standard features of religious or civic rituals in antiquity was the use of incense and other fragrant materials. Religious processions, the arrival of an important dignitary, the triumphal return of a Roman general, and so on, were all occasions on which such aromatics might be used. In describing the triumphal procession of Aemelius Paulus, Plutarch tells us that "every temple was open and filled with garlands and incense."[26] Continuing the image of the Roman triumph, Paul portrays his crushed and vanquished apostolic existence as the means through which the aroma of the crucified Christ is mediated to those around him. Paradoxically, God's strength is most potently displayed through Paul's weakness. Already the apostle is preparing the ground for his startling

---

[25] Richard L. Pratt, Jr, vol. 7, I & II Corinthians, Holman New Testament Commentary, 320-21 (Nashville, TN: Broadman & Holman Publishers, 2000).

[26] Aemelius Paulus 32.

declaration in 12:10, "For when I am weak, then I am strong."

For we are to God the aroma of Christ among those who are being saved and those who are perishing (2:15). Embedded within the imagery of the triumphal procession is an allusion to the Levitical sacrifices of the Old Testament, where the terms *euōdia* (NIV "fragrance") and *osmē* (NIV "aroma") combine to refer to a sacrificial "aroma pleasing to the LORD" (Lev. 2:2, 12; 6:14, etc.). As elsewhere (e.g., Col. 1:24), Paul portrays his apostolic suffering as an extension of the suffering of Christ, and he will make this point more explicitly in 4:10: "We always carry around in our body the death of Jesus."

To the one we are the smell of death; to the other, the fragrance of life (2:16). Although the transitions between metaphors is abrupt, Paul returns to the spectacle of the triumph and notes the differing effects the aroma-filled parade route would have on those involved. For the cheering crowds, the victorious soldiers, and the gloating general, this was the sweet fragrance of victory. But to the unfortunate captives destined for the auctioneer's block or execution in the forum, this was the scent of death itself.

Unlike so many, we do not peddle the word of God for profit (2:17). Preaching the gospel for mere financial gain has been a problem from the earliest days of the Christian movement. Already by the time of the *Didache* (ca. A.D. 80–150) Christian communities were exhorted to judge itinerant Christian teachers with reference to their desire for monetary gain: "And when the apostle leaves, he is to take nothing except bread until he finds his next night's lodging. But if he asks for money he is a false prophet."[27] ...

Paul's point is that unlike so many who proclaim their "religion" for a price, he and his companions preach Christ for altruistic reasons.[28]

While it is true that this sort of evangelism, house to house, can be very trying, it also brings the greatest joys at the same time as well. Imagine that you are in a desert, walking, staggering alone, dehydrated, parched, gasping for air, and you come up a source of water over the next dune that you cross. The relief, the joy, the gratitude, the thoughts that you had for miles of walking, where you had considered, "I will just lie down, and never wake again," are all gone, as you fall to the ground in tears, grateful that you never gave up! One may be out in this evangelistic work for months, growing ever tired from coming across the ungrateful, the critics, the sarcastic, the short tempered, the uninterested, and the opposer, when they finally come upon the smiling face that invites them in their home. They get you something cold to drink, and they then sit and listen to the message that you have brought, and you can see the light in their eyes, the hunger and thirst to know more.

---

[27] Did. 11:6.

[28] Clinton E. Arnold, Zondervan Illustrated Bible Backgrounds Commentary Volume 3: Romans to Philemon., 207-08 (Grand Rapids, MI: Zondervan, 2002).

The same difficult time as is found in the above plays out, but this time, it is the Bible critic, who lets you in, and offers you a drink. They let you share the Good News that you have brought, patiently waiting their turn to communicate. Unknown to you, they have been reading one Bible critic book after another. You pause after leaving them with a question, and then they pounce on you like a lion after his prey, with one question after another. You can be one of two people: either **(1)** the prepared or **(2)** the unprepared.

As the **unprepared**, you are struck by the fact that you have been carrying a Bible for many years, and are unable to defend the very book you call the Word of God. You are hurt by the fact that you have learned how to share your faith, but have never considered how you might defend your faith. As the **prepared**, you hold up your hand, the young mind in front of you comes to a halt, and you say, "I see that you have been doing much reading. I am very pleased that you have some interest in the Bible." You go on, saying, "We can address every one of your concerns, one at a time, and this approach will work best as we resolve one, and then move onto the next." He agrees that this is the best approach.

He leans in, eyes as bright from the start, and argues that **"if there was** an Adam and Eve, and an Abel who was now dead, so, where did Cain get his wife?"

You respond with, "If one were to read a little further along, they would come to the realization that Adam had a son named Seth; it further adds that Adam "became father to sons *and daughters.*" (Genesis 5:4) Adam lived for a total of 800 years after fathering Seth, giving him ample opportunity to father many more sons and daughters. Therefore, it could be that Cain married one of his sisters. If he waited until one of his brothers and sisters had a daughter, he could have married one of his nieces once she was old enough."

You continue, saying that "In the beginning, humans were closer to perfection; this explains why they lived longer and why at that time there was little health risk of genetic defects in the case of children born to closely related parents, in contrast to how it is today. As time passed, genetic defects increased and life spans decreased. Adam lived to see 930 years. Yet Shem, who lived after the Flood, died at 600 years, while Shem's son Arpachshad only lived 438 years, dying before his father died. Abraham saw an even greater decrease in that he only lived 175 years, while his grandson Jacob was 147 years when he died. Thus, due to increasing imperfection, God prohibited the marriage of closely related people under the Mosaic Law because of the likelihood of genetic defects. (Lev. 18:9.)"

Undaunted by your response, he realizes you have offered him a reasonable answer, but he moves on. He asks, "If we read at Exodus 4:21 that God is here **hardening Pharaoh's heart**, what exactly makes Pharaoh responsible for the decisions he makes?"

You respond with saying, "This is actually a prophecy. God knew that what he was about to do would contribute to a stubborn and obstinate Pharaoh, who was going to be unwilling to change or give up the Israelites so they could go off to worship their God. Therefore, this is not stating what God is going to do; it is prophesying that Pharaoh's heart will harden because of the actions of God. The fact is, Pharaoh allowed his own heart to harden because he was determined not to agree with Moses' wishes or accept Jehovah's request to let the people go. Moses tells us at Exodus 7:13 (UASV) that 'Pharaoh's heart was hardened, and he would not listen to them, as Jehovah had said.' Again, at 8:15 we read, 'When Pharaoh saw that there was a respite, he hardened his heart and would not listen to them, as Jehovah had said.' "

This goes on for some time, one question after the other. Over time though, you could feel that he was losing steam, and he was slowing with less and less eagerness. Soon, he was leaning in, because he wanted to hear what you had to say, and was no longer dismissive of your reasonable, logical responses. Before you left, he was now asking you, "Can you come back, as I want to hear more about your message?" Yes, you were **used by God**, as you defended the Word; you defended the faith, and you were used by God to open the eyes of the blind, because you listened to the inspired Word of God. (Prov. 2:1-6; Josh. 1:8; Ps. 1:1-3; 1 Pet. 3:15; Jude 1:3, 22-23) You may feel that it takes too much time to be this **prepared** as opposed to the shameful embarrassment of being **unprepared**. This could not be further from the truth, as it only takes one hour a day of personal Bible study, six days a week, Monday through Saturday.

Now, what other ways can we share our faith with our community?

Street Witnessing

The primary method of sharing the Good News in the community is by going house-to-house. However, maybe you are unable to find certain ones at home, because they work a shift at the time you are able to go out. Then, some people live in gated communities, which you cannot get access to, because there is a restriction against the house-to-house work.

In addition, some high-rise apartment buildings do not allow entry but to those that live, or if you are invited, meaning that you are cut off from sharing the message with these as well. This is why witnessing on the street can be quite effective, as we must reach everyone. The most important thing to keep in mind is that this should be carried out in the most respectful way possible, never being aggressive, or have any showy display, such as loud talk, or especially yelling and screaming.

Informal Witnessing

This is sharing the Good News with people as you come across them in the community: the store, doctor's office, public transportation, and so on. We are actively to seek out these ones in our everyday activities, such as a fellow employee, a fellow student at school, being served by a waitress at a restaurant, visiting a friend, and so on. All of these are acts of what is known as an informal evangelism. (John 4:7-15) These are unplanned but not unprepared occasions where we have an opportunity to share some form of Christian teaching with another person.

This is an effective tool in your evangelism toolbox, in helping them to hear the Good News of God's kingdom. As this facet of witnessing is usually quite brief, one must be prepared with what they might say, and have a Bible tract with them, getting something into their hands before parting ways. On that tract should be a way for them to get back with you if they so desire. If you feel things went well enough in this short exchange, you may ask them for some contact information. It takes a lot of courage to approach complete strangers, but it is our love for them, which moves us to buy out the time in this sort of evangelism. It is God, who gives "us a spirit not of fear but of power and love and self-control. Therefore, do not be ashamed of the testimony about our Lord." (2 Tim. 1:7, 8)

Telephone Witnessing

Small groups of congregation members put to use a reverse phone directory (lists phone numbers by addresses), and go to a small call center that has been set up in the congregation. This is great for getting to people that live in gated communities, or in high-rise apartments that you do not have access to otherwise. Just because we are not face-to-face, does not mean that it is any less effective. In fact, it may be easier on both of you, because there seems to be less stress. The Christian making the call can have notes in front of him, as well as any kind of research tool, enabling him to field questions. It could be set up so that it works off a desktop computer, with a headset that also has a microphone, leaving the hands free. This is certainly an effective tool.

Remember, this is not the primary way to reach people, but is only a tool for those that you cannot find at home in your community (i.e., the reverse phone directory). The headset should be set up on the computer, so that you can have a splitter plugged in, and multiple people can listen. This way you can train ones, who have done this form of witnessing. However, it would be best if two people at a time take a call (Luke 10:1). One is the person, who is trying to reach the person, they could not find at home, and the other is the helper, who looks up information or takes notes based on the conversation.

Telemarketing has caused people to shy away from taking calls from anyone they do not know. Therefore, it is best to show feelings of kindness, pleasantness, and tactfulness with your voice. Do not speak too loud, and do not speak too low. You may mention at the outset that you are not selling anything. Use your name, letting them know that you live in their community, and were sharing one Scripture with them and their neighbors. Rather than ask if you can read a Scripture, after stating that is why you have called, just jump to the Scripture, fully citing it and reading it. After reading it, ask a very short open-ended question about the Scripture. If he or she shares their thoughts, keep your word by offering a short comment and closing out the call. Before hanging up, ask if you may call back this time next week, so you can briefly share another Scripture. On the third or fourth week of doing this, you can begin to engage in more of a conversation. Remember, you will eventually want to visit them in their home, and start a Bible study with them.

Witnessing by Writing Letters

Again, this would be great for getting to people that live in gated communities, or in high-rise apartments that you do not have access to otherwise. Moreover, this would be the approach for one who has a physical disability that keeps them from going out into their community. You can write letters to people within your community, sharing a short biblical thought with them, and enclosing a tract as well. This is an easier form of evangelism, because to can take your time, to get your words just right, and there is no pressure.

Returning to Evangelize Again

You have made the initial contact with a new believer. In the initial conversation, you have planted a couple biblical truths, so you need to return to water these, enabling them to grow. (1 Cor. 3:6-8) You now need to get some kind of contact information: phone number, email, or address. You can leave them with a biblical question to ponder, stating what would be the best way to get back with them. Keep in mind that while it may not seem like there is much interest; life is always influencing a person's worldview. Moreover, it is your job to cultivate interest as well.

Remember, your end objective is to start a Bible study with ones who are interested. You are always in search of those, who will be receptive to a Bible study. (Matt. 10:11) If you do have one who gives you their contact information, make sure that you get back with them in about a week, because you do not want their interest to fade. In planning your phone call if it was a phone number, or your email, or a visit to their home, make sure you prepare well. Before leaving the first time, you may have left her or him with a thought provoking question, which you will be addressing this second time. You should have written their name down, and some interesting information that you gleaned from your initial conversation. Use that to show interest in the return.

Your love of God and neighbor keeps this person on your mind until your next contact with them. Once you are on the line with them, or at their home, use their name; try to make the same connection you had the first time around, by spending some time, showing a genuine interest in them. Make them the center of attention by asking open-ended questions that they can answer at length, and be an **active**

listener (more on active listening later). In other words, do not be thinking about your next comment or question when the person is talking. An active listener will look at the person while they are talking (not a constant stare, but periodic), and they will move their head in agreement or in word, to let the speaker know that you are listening. If possible, show that you are empathetic to what they are saying, by responding with something like, "I have felt that way before, too." It is permissible to ask short clarifying questions as well, which is another way to help the speaker know you are interested.

Remember that your second contact is all about them, with your interjecting some Scripture in, so they remember, it is God's Word that brought you to them. On the second visit, share at least one Scripture, getting their insights as to what they think, tactfully offering the correct interpretation if they are off the mark. With each visit, keep in mind that you are working toward starting a Bible study with them, and inviting them to a congregation meeting. On the visit where you bring up the possibility of a Bible study, pull out the book you intend to use, and hand it to them. Explain to them that the study is free of charge, something that takes place once a week, in the convenience of their home if they like, for 30-60 minutes. Have them turn to the Table of Contents in the book and walk through some of the things you would be covering. Again, it is our job to cultivate interest in others. Conversation skills are not something that can be taken in by reading some rules and principles. No, they are learned by implementing those rules and principles repeatedly, until you become skillful. The first time you find an uninterested person, and you develop interest by way of your conversation skills, it will bring you real joy that you have never felt in your life.

Witnessing to Strangers at Meetings

You should be alert to noticing any new faces at the meetings, going up to them and introducing yourself. You should get to know them as you express that you genuinely hope to see them again, befriending yourself to them. Keep in mind that, if everyone assumes that someone else will carry out this form of witnessing, no one will end up doing it, leaving a new believer feeling unwanted.

Witnessing by Our Conduct

Either our conduct can help us to shine light on the truth of God's Word, or we can bring reproach on it. (Titus 2:10) If others outside of your congregation have something good to say about your work in the community, this brings honor and glory to God. (1 Pet. 2:12) This can bring new ones to your congregation, because of what they have heard.

Effective Use of Bible Tracts

If you are to engage another in an effective conversation, you have to get the conversation started. Like a good book, or a great magazine article, the beginning will determine if you keep going. What you want to do is get the person's attention immediately. You introduce yourself, and a very brief statement that you are talking to people in your community about the Bible, and then offer a tract visually. Most Bible tracts have two things in common: (1) the titles are designed to peak interest, and (2) the cover image is designed to leap off the page at you, making you want to read it.

Another facet of offering tracts is their size. In a world where it seems that no one has time for anyone else, these short Bible tools can have an impact. When you offer something with a title and image that will capture the interest of the listener, your success is bound to increase. The best way to offer the tracts is to pick out about 4-6 of your best ones, with eye-opening titles and images. Either spread them out as you would a hand of cards, and show them, or preferably place them in the hands of the person, and ask, "Which one would you like?" Now, they are in his hands, he is looking through them, settles on one, and says, "This one."

Now, of course, you will have read every tract you offer very studiously yourself. Therefore, you will have a question lined up that highlights the substance of the tract he chose. After asking for it, open the tract, read that paragraph that answers the question, and the Scripture that is cited in it from your Bible. If the listener is very conversational, discuss more of the tract, giving him many opportunities to share in the conversation. Before closing the conversation, let him know that you would love to talk again, and write your contact information on the back of the tract, and ask him for his email or phone number.

CHAPTER 5 Other Methods of Evangelism

Benjamin Cocar

The method by which we evangelize another will be different depending on the person, the culture, the age, and their ability to comprehend and understand what we are saying. The biblical information is what will not change, it is important that it be what the author meant by the words that he used, as would have been understood by his audience.

Mass Evangelism

This method of evangelism emphasizes the preaching the Gospel to many people at one time. This kind of evangelism requires one or more evangelists, men with a special call to be evangelists (Eph. 4:11). The meetings should be well organized by one or more local churches, churches that invite unconverted people from their community. It is an effort that should involve all the members of the church. The local radio and TV stations should be announcing the event. Good music is essential for this type of evangelism. Besides the evangelist, the singers and a host of personnel, lay evangelists should be at hand. The church should specially train them for the event. They should be placed all over the place and they must be ready to help those who answer the invitation. They should walk with them; pray with them, encouraging and explaining them what they are doing.

Age-group Evangelism

This method concentrates on age related groups of people. Two of the groups that are the most evangelized are:

1. children--child evangelism,
2. youth--Youth for Christ.org.

This method is good because it addresses specific age-groups with specific needs, desires, interests. Although it is very good, this method is not inclusive enough.

Evangelists that are working with specific age-groups must study the specifics of the age-group with which they are dealing.

Radio/television Evangelism

This method is not available in all the parts of the world, but where it is available it should be used, because it reaches more people than any other method. The waves of radio and TV can penetrate homes that personal evangelists can never penetrate.

Although in recent years, many bad things have been said about the "electronic evangelism," it is still used around the world. Eternity will reveal the real impact of the electronic evangelism. The evangelists that preach on TV or on the radio should be very precise in their message, brief, and should be warm. Being warm in front of the microphone is not so easy, but they should view the potential masses of people listening to the message.

TransWorld Radio penetrated through many iron curtains, and walls with the Gospel's message; the same is true about Free Europe Radio, Back to the Bible, Radio Bible Class, HCJB of Quito, Ecuador, etc.

In the 10/40 window there are hundreds of radio programs that propagate the Word of God, the only way available today for most of the people living in that part of the world.

Bible Camp Evangelism

This is definitely an American feature. Concentrated effort is joined to the relaxation of camp life. The free-and-easy atmosphere tends to break down barriers and induce frank discussions. The Bible camp presents a challenge to the leaders and to the Christians attending, for unless the living corresponds to the teaching, the effect on the non-Christian can be disastrous. Many good intentions ended in sin and shame in too many Bible camps. The leaders of the different groups should be aware of potential trouble, and they should prepare the members of their groups to handle all kind of situation.

The material the Bible camp uses should be well prepared, should be attractive, easy to read and understand.

Movies

Many churches used this method with great results. The public generally accepted the Gospel science films of the Moody Institute of Science, and missionaries are using them in many countries. Movies can be used in a very effective way in home Bile studies.

We should practice caution. Short movies with a clear message should be presented, and then the host should offer time for questions and answers, and for prayer.

Internet evangelism

The electronic mail connects millions of people around the world. The business world is taking full advantage of this new method of doing business "on-line." Christians have already hundreds of "home-pages" promoting their churches, Christian organization, tapes, books, etc. Evangelism should use this new tool to its full potential. Open and polite discussion can present great opportunities to introduce the good news via Internet.

There are many "chat groups" where people can "talk" with others about their interests. The Christian's interests are Christ's interests, to bring the whole world to know Him, to receive His grace.

CHAPTER 6 Difficulties in Evangelism

Benjamin Cocar

If evangelism had been an easy task by this time, we could have seen the whole world evangelized, the task completed, and Christ on the clouds to take His Church up to Heaven. Yet it was not and it is not an easy task, this is why we are not send alone. Nevertheless, He gave us the Spirit. The Holy Spirit will help us in overcoming all the difficulties in evangelism.

Intimidation/fear

Most of the Christians have some kind of fear of evangelism, although most of them never evangelized . . . because of fear. There is a kind of "holy fear" when we do evangelism, and having it in our hearts is only normal, but when it becomes so strong that prevents us to tell others about Christ, then it is wrong.

Some of us are timid souls by nature, but this can and must be overcome if we want to be effective witnesses.

A good example is Peter. He made great claims of allegiance to Jesus but he folded under pressure. His desire to support Jesus was noble, but the circumstances of that fateful night around the campfire pushed Him into denying he was even associated with his Lord (Luke 22:54-62). Nevertheless, after the Holy Spirit came upon the disciples, Peter had the boldness to preach Jesus to a great multitude of people. The fear is there, but the Holy Spirit will overcome it. However, keep this in mind; the Holy Spirit can only draw on what is available to be drawn. In other words, if we have very little or no Bible knowledge, because we have failed to buy out the time to study God's Word, the Holy Spirit can call nothing back to our mind, because there is nothing to call back.

The fear of man's opinion about us, the fear of being rejected, the fear of being ridiculed is unhealthy, is destructive, and by the power of the Holy Spirit we have to overcome it. We have nothing to be afraid of, nothing to be ashamed of. The Gospel that we have is the power of God. Pray and ask God to deliver you from fear. However, have a daily Bible reading schedule, personal Bible study time, prepare for Christian meetings, and have regular church attendance. Always remember whose interests we are representing. We are His ambassadors, we have the Holy Spirit as our Helper, and our society must not intimidate us. We might be in minority, but we have God on our side, and any minority, with the addition of God is always the majority![29]

Unpreparedness of Mind and Heart

Another difficulty in evangelism is the unpreparedness of the mind and heart of many Christians. Personal evangelists or mass evangelists try to do the "work of an evangelist" with their minds and hearts totally unprepared.

People that move in other countries learn the language of the country if they want to survive, and to communicate with the people of their adoptive country. The Christian should learn to speak the language of his generation to be able to tell the Gospel. The message of the Gospel did not change

---

[29] Ashamed of the Gospel, John MacArthur, Crossway Books, 1993!

from the beginning, but the communication style changed throughout history. The Christian should not only hold to the basics, scriptural principles of the Christian faith, but he has to tell these unchanging truths into the generation in which it is living. Every generation of Christians had this problem of learning how to speak meaningfully to its own age. They do not know how to speak the language of their generation mainly because they fail to understand the thought-form of that particular generation. In preparing our minds for evangelism, we must understand the thought-form of our present generation. Paul sets an example in Acts 17. He saw the things that were present in Athens, he listened, (another technique that we did not learn, to listen!), to the ideas they promoted, and from the inscription on an altar he went on and preached Jesus. The results were not great, but this is not our concern. He called us to preach the Gospel, and remember, the results are in His hands.

Our minds must be always prepared for the task of evangelism by knowing the message of the cross well. We have to know the plan of salvation well.

As Christians in the last decade of the twentieth century, we must know the Christian doctrines, God, Jesus Christ, the Holy Spirit, the Bible, man, Satan, Sin, Salvation, Church, Rapture, Judgment. Keep in mind, the above subject areas are the foundation, the beginning, the basics of what any Christian needs to know.

Every Christian should study three books after this publication: <u>THE EVANGELISM HANDBOOK: How All Christians Can Effectively Share God's Word in Their Community</u>. Two other books need to be studied through as well. You need to study a book on Biblical interpretation. We highly recommend Basic Bible Interpretation by Roy B. Zuck (January 1991).[30] This is absolutely the best book on the Basics of Biblical Interpretation. In addition, you need to study a book on the basics of Biblical doctrines. I recommend AMG Concise Bible Doctrines (AMG Concise Series) by Elmer Towns (July 5, 2006)[31]

Therefore, the congregation, or you as an individual, should study the following books:

(1) Basic Bible Interpretation

(2) Concise Bible Doctrines

(3) The Evangelism Handbook[32]

(4) The Christian Apologist[33]

The Condition of the Unconverted

Another difficult hindrance in evangelism is the condition of the lost person. Paul writes about the unconverted and he tells that those without Christ cannot understand the spiritual things (1 Cor. 2:14).[34] The things you want to tell Him about

---

[30] ISBN: 978-0781438773

[31] ISBN: 978-0899576954

[32] ISBN-13: 978-0615877938

[33] ISBN-13: 978-0692303153

[34] It is not that unbelievers (unconverted) cannot understand God's Word; otherwise, why evangelize them. It is that some unbelievers see the Word of God as foolish and reject it. For a deeper understanding of 1 Corinthians 2:14, please read, **The Work of the Holy Spirit (esp. Biblical Interpretation)**

http://www.christianpublishers.org/holy-spirit-the-work-of

salvation, new life, and new birth seemed like foolishness to Him. Nicodemus did not understand the new birth notion (John 3:4, 9-10).[35] Did Jesus simply abandon Nicodemus? No. He continued to bring an example that Nicodemus knew Moses' brazen snake, and paralleled that example with His own sacrificial death, (John 3:14-16).

The lost man is in a state of war with God; there is enmity between Him and God. The moment you present the Gospel to those with an unreceptive heart, something reacts in him against all that you presented. He hates God, and most of them think that God hates them too. The way Jesus spoke to Nicodemus, gives us a good pattern to follow in our task of evangelism. If the people we are presenting the plan of salvation reject God, and many will, we can bring John 3:16 into focus . . . "God loved the world to the extreme, he gave his only begotten Son . . ." This God loves the world, He wants them back to Him.

The condition of the lost person should not be a barrier for the evangelist. We know that our work is in a hostile environment, we work on the enemy's field, but we have the God of the universe on our side, we represent the King of Kings, and the Holy Spirit works through us. We have to try to win people as friends, and then win those friends for Jesus.

Look at Jonathan's friendship to David as a model. Be first to show friendship. Remember his or her name. Be genuinely interested in him. Put him or her first. Jonathan

---

[35] Actually, it isn't that Nicodemus did not understand the illustration of the new birth per se, because that was a common concept within Rabbinical Judaism. It was that he did not accept that there was some need for Jews to be reborn spiritually. Thus, he saw what Jesus was saying as foolish.

was a prince, but when he saw David, he proved himself as a faithful friend even against his father' hate for David, 1 Sam 18-29. We can invite our friends to a Bible study in our home, or another Christian's home. Try to make them feel accepted, and be sensitive to their eventual questions.

Keep in mind, as we grow in our evangelism skills we will be better able to ascertain, who has a receptive heart and who does not. We need to learn such skills as overcoming comments that are dismissive (2 Cor. 10:4-5), reasoning and explaining from the Scriptures (Acts 17:2-3), being prepared to make a defense to anyone who asks you for a reason (1 Pet. 3:15), helping those who have begun to doubt, and contending for the faith. (Jude 1:3, 22-23) Nevertheless, we need to identify those that do not have a receptive heart, because our time could be better spent with one, who has a receptive heart. Having said all of this, we still deal with the unreceptive with gentleness and respect, seasoning our words with salt.

Colossians 4:6 English Standard Version (ESV)

⁶ Let your speech always be gracious, seasoned with salt, so that you may know how you ought to answer each person.

CHAPTER 7 Evangelism Through the Local Church

Benjamin Cocar

Every believer belongs to a local church, and God called everyone to do evangelism. Each should do personal evangelism, but the church as a body, what is her role?

In Acts 2, we witness the birth of the Christian Church, and moments after the coming of the Holy Spirit, the new organism was doing evangelism, i.e., corporate evangelism. All the disciples praised God, and when provoked, Peter stood up and preached Jesus. The people responded, and he gave them the solution, "Repent, and be baptized, every one of you . . . " Acts 2:38.

Jesus spoke to his followers and told them that they are the salt and the light of this world, Matthew 5:13-16, and as such, we should let our light shine in this dark world.

The regular Meetings

The worship service should be a place for believers and unbelievers to meet God. Every pastor should include some kind of evangelistic effort in every meeting of the church. There is no meeting that has only believers present. Always someone will be there who needs the Gospel. By giving an invitation or not, the pastor should arrange for the unsaved that might be there. The same truth applies to every department of the local church, Sunday Schools classes, women's groups, men's groups, children, youth etc.

Gospel presentation is essential in every activity of the church. The great commission means to make disciples, and to make disciples, the church must evangelize. However, every member is obligated regardless the meeting to attempt to introduce themselves to any new ones.

Evangelistic Program

We find that every church, regardless of denomination, has some sort of Bible study class, which is broken up into ages, or level f difficulty, or some other fashion. This is commendable. However, almost no church has a regular evangelism class. If we are to have a successful evangelism program, every church must have a consistent regular evangelism program.

Excursion on Evangelism Program

The Evangelism Handbook by Edward D. Andrews

Course Schedule

Date: Each week of the course schedule will have a section of a chapter assigned. Each student should prepare that section at home beforehand, by studying through this section, highlighting or underlining the answers to the review questions, looking up all cited Scriptures (unless they are quoted), and doing the course project.

Reading and Studying: The students will read and study the assigned material for the coming week at home beforehand, which includes the review question(s) and the course project, even though the project may not have been assigned to them. This section will be covered before the school course projects get underway.

Review Questions: As opposed to placing review questions at the end of a chapter, they are placed throughout, so the student will know what portion goes with what review questions. The student should read the question(s), and then read the section that it is applicable to them, which may vary in length. Then, read the question again, before highlighting or underlining the answers.

Evangelism Program Director: The one taking the lead should be a person that has extensive Bible knowledge, such as a completed associates or bachelor in biblical studies, as well as having a gift in the area of effective communication and teaching skills.[36] The director is to produce the course schedule each time the program begins. After the student has carried out the course project in front of the congregation, before leaving the stage, he will receive constructive feedback.

Evangelism Program Assistant Director: The assistant director should be a congregation member in good standing, living an exemplar Christian life. He too should have some background in having

---

[36] The author of this publication is also the president of Biblical Training Academy; which is designed as a complement of this book. We highly recommend the 45-hour certificate in Biblical Studies from Biblical Training Academy. http://www.biblicaltrainingacademy.com/

studied the deeper things, as well as exemplary communication and teaching skills.[37] The assistant director can be used to produce the course schedule. He is to hand out the course project to the students ahead of time, giving them an opportunity to prepare for the upcoming class. He will assign others as replacements, if the student cannot make the meeting to fulfill their project. He is to offer private counsel to any student that has questions about their project beforehand, or after it has been given.

Course Project: The assistant director will hand out course project four weeks before they are to be carried out by the student. Course projects are to be done on stage in front of the congregation. After the project is completed, the student will remain on stage to receive feedback from the director, so the entire congregation can benefit from this counsel. While the director will go over constructive counsel, he is to offer it in a manner that is beneficial, and spiritually uplifting. Below is an example of a course schedule, followed by directions for each type of course project.

---

[37] The author of this publication is also the president of Biblical Training Academy; which is designed as a complement of this book. We highly recommend the 48-hour certificate in Biblical Studies from Biblical Training Academy. http://www.biblicaltrainingacademy.com/

COURSE SCHEDULE
EVAN 101

Textbook: Evangelical Handbook, by Edward D. Andrews

Date	Reading and Studying	Review Questions	Course Projects
January 01, 2015	Evangelism Handbook **CH**. 1 **pp**. 19-25	Review Questions	Student(s) name and project
January 08, 2015	Evangelism Handbook **CH**. 2 **pp**. 27-33	Review Questions	The Student(s) will carry out the chapter project.
January 15, 2015	Evangelism Handbook **CH**. 3 **pp**. 63-80	Review Questions	The Student(s) will carry out the chapter project.
January 22, 2015	Evangelism Handbook **CH**. 4 **pp**. 81-112	Review Questions	The Student(s) will carry out the chapter project.
January 29, 2015	Evangelism Handbook **CH**. 5 **pp**. 113-140	Review Questions	The Student(s) will carry out the chapter project.

The schedule can be made up a month at a time, or it could be every three months, or longer. It should have enough time that will allow the student the opportunity to prepare well.

Course Project A: Biblical Interpretation Explained

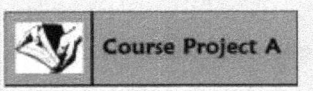

Biblical Interpretation: After reading a text, such as **Joshua 1:1-9**,[38] The student will explain the results of the steps that he followed:

Step 1: What is the historical setting and background for the author of the book and his audience? Who wrote the book? When and under what circumstances was the book written? Where was the book written? Who were the recipients of the book? Was there anything noteworthy about the place of the recipients? What is the theme of the book? What was the purpose for writing the book?

Step 2a: What would this text mean to the original audience? (The meaning of a text is what the author meant by the words that he used, as should have been understood by his readers.)

Step 2b: If there are any words in this section that one does not understand, or that stand out as interesting words that may shed some insight on the meaning, look them up in a word dictionary, such as *Mounce's Complete Expository Dictionary of Old and New Testament Words*.

Step 2c: After reading your section from the three Bible translations, doing a word study, write down what you think the author meant. Then, pick up a trustworthy commentary, like Holman Old or New Testament commentary volume, and see if you have it correct.

Step 3: Explain the original meaning in one or two

---

[38] Again, any verse that this book recommends in a course project, can be set aside by your director the second time through the book.

> sentences, preferably one. Then, take the sentence or two and place it in a short phrase.
>
> **Step 4**: Now, consider their circumstances, the reason for it being written, what it meant to them, and consider examples from our day that would be similar to theirs, which would fit the pattern of meaning. What **implications** can be drawn from the original meaning?
>
> **Step 5**: Find the pattern of meaning, the "thing like these," and consider how it could apply in our modern day life. How should individual Christians today live out the implications and principles?

Step 1: What is the historical setting and background for the author of the book and his audience? Who wrote the book? When and under what circumstances was the book written? Where was the book written? Who were the recipients of the book? Was there anything noteworthy about the place of the recipients? What is the theme of the book? What was the purpose for writing the book? The first step is observation, to get as close to the original text as possible. If one does not read Hebrew or Greek; then, two or three literal translations are preferred (ESV, NASB, and HCSB). The above Bible background information may seem daunting, but it can all be found in the Holman Bible Handbook or the Holman Illustrated Bible Dictionary.

Step 2a: What would this text mean to its original audience? (The meaning of a text is what the author meant by the words that he used, as should have been understood by his readers.) Once you have an understanding of step 1, **read** and reread your text in its context.[39] In most Bibles,

---

[39] Context is the verses that come before and after the text that we are considering.

there are indentations (breaks) where the subject matter changes. Look for the indentations that are before and after your text, and **read** and reread that whole section from three literal translations. If there are no indentations, read the whole chapter, and get a sense of where the breaks should be, that is, where the subject matter changes.

Step 2b: If there are any words in your section that you do not understand, or that stand out as interesting words that may shed some insight on the meaning, look them up in a word dictionary, such as *Mounce's Complete Expository Dictionary of Old and New Testament Words*. For example, if the text was Ephesians 5:14, one might ask what did Paul mean by "sleeper" in verse 14. If it was Ephesians 5:18, what does Paul mean by his use of the word "debauchery" in relation to "getting drunk with wine." I would recommend *Mounce's Complete Expository Dictionary of Old and New Testament Words* by William D. Mounce (Sept. 19, 2006) Do not buy the Amazon Kindle edition until they work out the minor difficulty. If you have Logos Bible Software, it would be good to add this book, if it did not come with your package.

Step 2c: After reading the section from the three Bible translations, doing a word study, write down what you think the author meant. Then, find a trustworthy commentary, like Holman Old or New Testament commentary volume, and see if you have it correct. It can be more affordable to buy one volume each time you are assigned a project, so that it is spread out over time. If you cannot afford each volume of these commentary sets, Holman has a one-volume commentary of the entire Bible. Check with your minister or pastor because he may allow you to take a volume home for your assignment.

Step 3: Explain the original meaning in one or two sentences, preferably one. Then, take the sentence or two and place it in a short phrase. If you look in the Bible for Ephesians chapter five, one will find verse 1-5 or 6 are marked off as a section, and the phrase that captures the sense of the meaning is, "imitators of God." Then, verses 6-16 of that same chapter can be broken down to "light versus darkness" or "walk like children of light."

Step 4: Now, consider their circumstances, the reason for it being written, what it meant to them, and consider examples from today that would be similar to that time, which would fit the pattern of meaning. What **implications** can be drawn from the original meaning? Part of this fourth step is making sure that one stays within the pattern of the original meaning when we determine any implications for us.

An example would be the admonition that Paul gave the Ephesian congregation at 5:18, "do not get drunk with wine." Was Paul talking about beer that existed then too? Surely, he was not explicitly referring to whiskey that was not invented until the 1800s. Yes, he refers to these others because they are implications that can be derived from the original meaning because of their likeness to that original meaning.

Step 5: Find the pattern of meaning, the "thing like these," and consider how it could apply in our modern day life. How should individual Christians today live out the implications and principles?

Course Project B Evangelism Opportunity

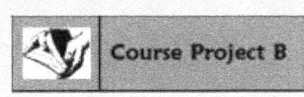

Evangelism Opportunity: This project will be set up so that a student is illustrating an example of an evangelism opportunity with someone in his or her community. It could be someone in the waiting room of a doctor's office, while in line at a store, on the phone at the call center in the congregation, while street witnessing, or any other informal opportunity. They will be assigned a subject matter here in *The Evangelism Handbook*, but the assistant director or director can change the subject matter based on the course schedule they have produced.

Evangelism opportunities are what we make, not situations that we just happen upon. It could be waiting in line at a store, passing someone on the street, a person who comes to repair something at our home, while in the waiting room at the doctor's office, family, friends, or a neighbor. We should be prepared for any opportunity that presents itself.

Course Project C Reading Skills

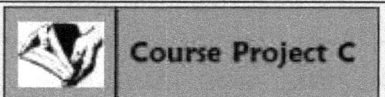

Reading Skills: The student will read a text, like James 1:1-27. This assignment will help improve our reading skills. When practicing before the meeting, read slowly enunciating every word meticulously, as well as adequate volume, and moving along at the appropriate pace. We need to read and speak words clearly, to not only be understood, but also leave an impression. In addition, read with precision, stopping or pausing for punctuations, as well as changing the tone of your voice, or adding the inflections that are required. It would be best to have someone follow along, letting you know if you make the appropriate pauses or inflections.

If we want to be taken serious by those that we speak to about our Christian faith, we will want to be serious about the need in becoming an effective reader. We need to be able to read the Bible if we are sharing a verse, or we may be reading from a book or Bible tract. If we stumble over the pronunciation of words, or skip over a section, or even slur our words, the person we are speaking with will not take us seriously. Would we entrust our life to a doctor, who is suggesting heart surgery, if he could not read well, or articulate his message? No. Therefore, why should the unbeliever trust their life to a person that speaks of life eternal, if they cannot read well, or articulate their message?

Course Project D: Reasoning From the Scriptures

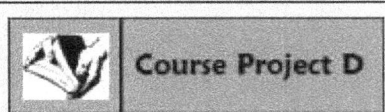

Reasoning From The Scriptures: The student will be assigned a subject, like infant baptism, and he or she will give a talk, reasoning from the Scriptures that it is biblical or not biblical.

1 Peter 3:15 English Standard Version (ESV)

¹⁵ but in your hearts honor Christ the Lord as holy, always being prepared to make a **defense** [apologia] to anyone who asks you for a reason for the hope that is in you; yet do it with gentleness and respect,

Here Peter is telling us that we are obligated to **defend the Christian hope**.

Philippians 1:7 English Standard Version (ESV)

⁷ It is right for me to feel this way about you all, because I hold you in my heart, for you are all partakers with me of grace, both in my imprisonment and in the **defense** [apologia] and confirmation of the gospel.

Philippians 1:16 English Standard Version (ESV)

¹⁶ The latter do it out of love, knowing that I am put here for the **defense** [apologia] of the gospel.

In both 1:1, and 16, Paul tells us that we are to **defend the Gospel**.

The Greek word behind the English '**defense**' is *apologia*, which is actually a legal term that refers to the defense of a defendant in court. The Christian defense of our hope and the Gospel, by extension, God's Word can be accomplished in one of two ways.

Negative Apologetics

In this, the Christian is like a defensive player in a ball game, who is trying to prevent the other player (Bible critic) from scoring points. The offensive player, the Bible critic will raise objections about some facet of Christianity. He might say, "The Bible is the word of man alone, it is not inspired by God; moreover, it is in fact full of contradictions and errors." Another comment might be his saying, "Jesus was just a human, not the divine Son of God, who was resurrected from the dead." Another might ask, "If there is truly a loving, all-powerful God, why does he allow such wickedness, pain, suffering and death?"

In our defense, we would offer reasons or evidence that the Bible critic's claims or accusations are not valid. In other words, we would debunk his claims or accusations. For example, in the above claim that the Bible is full of errors and contradictions, we would defend the Bible by showing that this really is not the case. We would explain that those are merely so-called errors and contradictions. We could say that there are thousands of difficulties in the Bible. I refer to them as Bible difficulties, because they are difficult for us to understand, because we are 2,000 to 3,500 years removed from dozens of different cultures, as well as three ancient languages: Hebrew, Aramaic and Greek. Moreover, persons with a lack of knowledge on how to read the text will come upon what they perceive to be errors and contradiction. Let us look at an example.

The Bible critic makes the claim, "Look at Jesus' comment about the mustard seed, 'The kingdom of heaven is like a grain of mustard seed that a man took and sowed in his field. It is the smallest of all seeds ...' Is the mustard seed the smallest? No. Then, Jesus was wrong, it is an error."

Negative apologetics would then demonstrate that that claim about Jesus being wrong is what is actually wrong. We would say, "Jesus was referring to a seed in ancient times that was very common to his audience, and was the tiniest to them. He was not giving a botany lesson. Jesus was absolutely accurate with his intended meaning."

Intended Meaning of Writer

First, the Bible student needs to understand the level that the Bible intends to be exact in what is written. If Jim told a friend that 650 graduated with him from high school in 1984, it is not challenged, because it is all too clear that he is using rounded numbers and is not meaning to be exactly precise. This is how God's Word operates as well.

Acts 2:41 (ESV): So those who received his word were baptized, and there were added that day about three thousand souls.

As you can see here, numbers within the Bible are often used with approximations. This is a frequent practice even today, in both written works and verbal conversation.

Acts 7:2-3 (ESV): Brothers and fathers, hear me. The God of glory appeared to our father Abraham when he was in Mesopotamia, before he lived in Haran, and said to him, "Go out from your land and from your kindred and go into the land that I will show you."

If you were to check the Hebrew Scriptures at Genesis 12:1, you would find that what is claimed to have been said by God to Abraham is not quoted word-for-word; it is simply a paraphrase. This is a normal practice within Scripture and in writing in general.

Numbers 34:15 (ESV): The two tribes and the half-tribe have received their inheritance beyond the Jordan east of Jericho, toward the sunrise.

Just as you would read in today's local newspaper, the Bible writer has written from the human standpoint, how it appeared to him. The Bible also speaks of "to the end of the earth" (Psalm 46:9), "from the four corners of the earth" (Isa. 11:12), and "the four winds of the earth" (Rev. 7:1). These phrases are still used today.

Burden of Proof

The burden of proof is a legal term. In a court trial, the prosecuting attorney is the one that brings charges against the defendant. He has the burden of proving those charges. The defendant is presumed to be innocent, and it is the prosecutor that has the obligation to give evidence that will persuade a jury that the presumed innocence is wrong, and the defendant is guilty of some crime. The Latin argument is, "the necessity of proof always lies with the person who lays charges." In other words, the defendant is presumed innocent, and he is not obligated to provide any evidence of his innocence. If the prosecutor fulfills his burden of proof, it means that he will have given enough evidence to prove his case, which then passes the burden of proof to the defendant, who must now use evidence, logic and reasoning, to demonstrate the evidence of the prosecutor is no evidence at all. As should be clear, the one who has the easiest time is the one presumed innocent or correct, while the more difficult time is with the one carrying the burden of proving their case.

Therefore, if you find yourself in a discussion with someone that is trying to make the claim that, say for example, the Jesus was not resurrected from the dead, he has the burden of disproving the historicity of Jesus' resurrection. Thus, negative apologetics is the easier form of apologetics, because all of the difficulty, the burden of proof is with the Bible critic. The Christian only needs to sit back and allow this one to lay out his evidence. Then, the Christian only has to demonstrate that his arguments fail to make his claim.

Positive Apologetics

Going back to our sports analogy, the Christian is playing offense, and the non-Christian is playing defense. In other words, the Christian is trying to score, while the unbeliever is trying to keep him from scoring. The burden of proof falls on the one making the claims. If the Christian is witnessing to another, he has the burden to prove what he says is so if asked for proof. As the one now trying to score points, the Christian needs to offer arguments, information, or explanations, which will help the unbeliever to the point of accepting the claim we have made.

Again, the one with the burden of proof finds himself in in the more difficult situation. If the Christian is witnessing about God, and the unbeliever asks for evidence of God's existence, the Christian is now obligated to offer proof for his claim that God exists. Depending on the person he is talking with, this is no easy task, because while there are arguments for the existence of God, they can get deep and complicated at times. Now, it becomes the unbelievers turn simply to disprove that the Christian has not made his case, that the Christians arguments are ineffective, and did not prove his claim of the existence of God.

It has become customary for the atheist to suggest that they never have the burden of proof, but rather the burden of proof always lies with the Christian. This is just not the case, and we need not do all the work in a discussion about our beliefs, the existence of God, the Bible, or anything else in our biblical worldview. The Latin argument is worth repeating, "The necessity of proof always lies with the person who lays charges."

End of Excursion[40]

Door-to Door Evangelism

Many churches organize door-to-door visitation programs. The church should instruct those who go door-to-door about their approach. In today's society, they bring

---

[40] Edward D. Andrews, *THE EVANGELISM HANDBOOK: How All Christians Can Effectively Share God's Word in Their Community* (Cambridge, OH: Christian Publishing House, 2013), pages 38-53.

many good and bad things to our doors. We must be careful how we go with the best news, the Gospel. The best idea is to have teams of two people each. At each door they knock, they should expect at least four kinds of answers:

(1) total rejection

(2) lack of interest, apathy

(3) Curiosity, some interest

(4) welcome

When rejected, apologize, and leave, but ask permission to give them a tract, if not, leave. If they show apathy, lack of interest, without being pushy, try to raise their interest in the eternal things, your church, the Gospel. Do not lose any opportunity for the gospel.

When welcomed, prudence must be the rule. Proceed with care, and present the simple plan of salvation, invite them to the church, leave some literature with them, and promise them a second visit.

Vacation Bible Schools

It requires much effort, good organization, but through the years, it produced results all over the country.

The church should plan well in advance, produce or purchase all the material they need, send invitations to all the families in the neighborhood, provide bus transportation, snacks, drinks.

The methods may vary from place to place, they may change from year to year, but principles never change. The principle of evangelism, which is "sharing Jesus Christ in the power of the Holy Spirit and leaving the results to God," never changes.

One preacher has defined evangelism as "simply, one beggar telling another beggar where to find bread." That principle of "giving away your faith" must not change. There is not a substitute for it. Some principles to be considered in evangelism are found in Colossians 1:27-29. Believers are to communicate the Gospel in such a way that it will show that they are informed, involved, and initiated.

Colossians 1:27-29 English Standard Version (ESV)

²⁷ To them God chose to make known how great among the Gentiles are the riches of the glory of this mystery, which is Christ in you, the hope of glory. ²⁸ Him we proclaim, warning everyone and teaching everyone with all wisdom, that we may present everyone mature in Christ. ²⁹ For this I toil, struggling with all his energy that he powerfully works within me.

CHAPTER 8 Everyday Informal Evangelism

Most of the Christians know their calling as children of God. It is not that they are not aware who they are, what is their call, but in the routine of their days, they pass by thousands of excellent opportunities for the Gospel. Why?

The opportunities are everywhere around us. People are hungry for love. They are waiting for someone to tell them of a better way of living, of something different, but the world catches the Christians in their dull pattern of activities, ignoring the great need and opportunity around them. Many think that the pastors, or those who have the call of evangelists must do the work of evangelizing the world, but the Bible does not teach that. Jesus was clear in His teaching that every believer must go and tell the good News.

Paul writes to the Corinthians telling them to spread the aroma of the knowledge of Jesus Christ, 2 Cor. 2:14-15. This is the most natural thing that the Christians can do, <u>live the life of Christ</u>!

Being salt of the earth, the Christian produces thirst in other people. It produces the appeal of the Gospel. An auto-mechanic can produce the appeal of the Gospel by treating every client with kindness, honesty, warmth. A young lady in the restaurant working as a server, can spread the aroma of Christ by being pleasant, ready to smile, and show the "peace of God that passes all understanding." There are so many Christians that become irritated, even angry when the line at the checking point is too long, and the cashier works too slowly. Everyone does, but the Christian can turn that situation in a great opportunity to spread the fragrance of the knowledge of Jesus.

Building bridges in our neighborhoods, building relationship with our neighbors, will help us in our daily work of evangelism.

In the neighborhood, the Christian must show that he cares, for people "do not care how much you know until they know how much you care!"

The way we drive in our neighborhoods can be a proof of what we are. The way we dress, we walk, and talk can and must be different. At the work place . . . a wrong attitude or wrong word can ruin thousands of opportunities for the Gospel. As Christians, we must try to turn every situation in our lives into opportunities to bring glory to God. On this matter, our editor Edward D. Andrews writes,

What is Informal Evangelism?

Informal witnessing means that we are prepared to give a witness about the good news at any time or place. We need to be (1) prepared, that is knowing the Bible well, (2) have some skills and practice in communicating our faith to others and defending God's Word, (3) relaxed, (4) friendly, and (5) unofficial. This is sharing the good news with people as you come across them in the community: the store, doctor's office, public transportation, and so on. We are actively to seek out these ones in our everyday activities, such as a fellow employee, a fellow student at school, being served by a server at a restaurant, visiting a friend, and so on. All of these are acts of what is known as an informal evangelism. (John 4:7-15) These are unplanned but not unprepared occasions where we have an opportunity to share some form of biblical truths (Christian teachings) with another.

The Evangelism Toolbox

This is an effective tool in your evangelism toolbox, in helping them to hear the Good News of God's kingdom. As this facet of witnessing is usually quite brief, one must be prepared with what they might say, and have a Bible tract with them, getting something into their hands before parting ways. On that tract should be a way for them to get back with you if they so desire. If you feel things went well enough in this short exchange, you may ask them for some contact information. It takes a lot of courage to approach complete strangers, but it is our love for them, which moves us to buy out the time in this sort of evangelism. It is God, who gives "us a spirit not of fear but of power and love and self-control. Therefore, do not be ashamed of the testimony about our Lord." 2 Tim. 1:7, 8

Informal evangelizing can be done in congenial, relaxed atmosphere, if one is confident in the lead of the Holy Spirit, and knowing they have prepared well. It can really be a friendly discussion, where much can be accomplished. In fact, we may encounter those that really have never had the privilege of conversing with a Christian, where they are able to get questions answered that may have been weighing on their heart. This informal conversation may have been started in the waiting room of the doctor's office, at a bus stop, on the bus, in a cab, on an airplane, even in line at a store.

| **Proverbs 15:7** English Standard Version (ESV)

⁷ The lips of the wise spread knowledge; not so the hearts of fools. | **Ecclesiastes 11:6** English Standard Version (ESV)

⁶ In the morning sow your seed, and at evening withhold not your hand, for you do not know which will prosper, this or that, or whether both alike will be good. |

When informally witnessing to another, keep your sentences few and short, designed specifically to peaking the interest of the other. This will move the other to ask questions about the faith, God's Word, life, and so on. In addition, everyone likes to share what they think, so we should use question in our informal witnessing. After they have had a chance to share their thoughts, we may offer the Bible's viewpoint. The main thing to keep in mind is, the need to always be discreet, respectful, and tactful. And here is where wisdom comes in, because we do not want to spend an exorbitant amount of time with those who are not receptive to the truth. Matthew 7:6

We can also informally witness at work too, by just casually bringing up things they may find interesting. This should not ever infringe on the companies time, or be repeated often to ones that are simply not interested. Small comments over time can build rapport, which can lead to discussion outside of work.

Just because we are informally witnessing to others, this does not mean that we are not prepared. You can have considered things to talk about, when the opportunity presents itself. You can carry tracts with you, but make sure you know the tracts well, and can offer them, knowing what they say. You can also have some Scripture to share that you have memorized. Take advantage of every moment that presents itself, as tomorrow could be the day we have all been waiting on.[41]

Literally hundreds of millions of people could be introduced to God's Word, if all Christians evangelized informally. As disciples of Jesus Christ, we must let our light shine at every opportunity. We may be hesitant at first or even failed miserably the first few times, but we cannot allow ourselves to be discouraged. In time, if we stay steadfast, we will eventually bear fruit. While skills will come in time, it is actually many occurrences, which will lead to some successes. Even if we have no Bible in hand, or we left our Bible tracts at home, or in the car, the opportunity should not be missed, as long as we have a voice with which we can speak. Because not all are making an opportunity, there is more for us to do, if the assignment Jesus gave is to be accomplished.

---

[41] Edward D. Andrews, *The Christian Evangelist: Go Therefore and Make Disciples In Your Own Community! Volume 1* (Cambridge, OH: Christian Publishing House, 2013), pages 135-138.

CHAPTER 9 Common Excuses from Both Sides

Benjamin Cocar

Excuses of the Believers

Even the best of men and women are prone to make excuses. A good excuse gives a person something to hide behind. Excuses come in all shapes and sizes, and if we look hard enough, we can find one that fits almost any situation. The amazing fact is that even people in the Bible that we admire, were sometimes guilty of hiding behind what to them sounded like a very legitimate excuse. Moses piled excuse after excuse to avoid the mission to Pharaoh (Ex. 3-4). Gideon felt the need of raising some excuse before he went to rescue Israel (Judges 6:15). Jeremiah, the weeping prophet, told God that he was a child (Jer.1: 6). Nevertheless, these ones carried out their assignments in faith, and were successful because God had their back.

Moses was afraid that his fellow Jews will not <u>believe</u> him that he cannot convince them that God sent him. Than he was afraid that they will not understand his words . . . excuses that are common among the Christians of our world. Many are afraid that their message is irrelevant, the ones he might tell the Good News might not believe . . . or maybe they feel that they are not eloquent speakers. Gideon wanted some visible manifestation of God's presence. He did not go to fight only after he was very sure that God could do things that are above the natural.

Jeremiah was frightened to death of the great task to preach God's message to an unrepentant generation, and tried to convinced God to find another man more experienced than him.

Still, in all the cases God did not pay too much attention to their excuses. He could find other people for those jobs, but He wanted them, and they did well, with His help!

The moment God called these men to His work. They all turned their thoughts on themselves. All began to look inward and dwell upon their own limitations. Rather than look at the Lord and dwell on the promises of His presence, His guidance, His power, they concentrated on their own weakness, their own lack of ability.

If the Christians get their eyes on themselves, they will fail.

Instead, they have to look upon Him who called them to do the work.

If all the Christians find excuses, who will proclaim the Gospel? Paul did not find excuses, he was eager to preach the Gospel, but Paul is gone, who is doing now the job of telling the Good News? We, the generation of Christians that did not suffer the things Paul suffered to preach the Gospel, we have to share the good news. Our generation has the possibilities that no other generation had. "God did not call me to preach," someone might say. Nevertheless, are we not called to shine our light into this dark world? Do we need a special call for that? "I am too young or too old," others might say. Jeremiah complained that he was but a child, and God did not take that as a valid excuse. Caleb, Joshua,

Daniel and John the Apostle were all old people, but that did not stop them to be great lights for God.

"I am too busy," some Christian could complain. Busy with what? With the work of the Lord? Reevaluate your priorities and you will discover that you have exactly 24 hours every day. At least 10% belong to the Lord. Do not rob Him.

Excuses of the Unbeliever

The excuses of the believers are many, but those of the unbelievers are so many that including them all is hard. Every person has its own set of excuses when it comes to the spiritual things. In Luke 14:15-20, we read about some people invited to a banquet, but what did they do? They attempted to beg off. Some of them just bought some stocks. They have to watch and see how they go. Some invested in some machinery for their farm, and seeing how they work is necessary. Another one just got married, and the honeymoon must be first. Excuses are many.

1. This is not for me.

Many people reject the Gospel believing that this is not for them. They are well to do in their positions and they just do not feel that this is for them.

    a. show them Romans 3:23, <u>all</u> have sinned,

    b. show then Romans 6:23, the wages of sin is <u>death</u>

Ask them if they can exclude themselves from <u>all</u>, and ask them if they like the result of their sin. If they are honest, they will recognize that the Gospel is for them.

2. I cannot give up my sins.

    a. ask Him if he wants to be free from sin, John 3:19

    b. show Him that Christ is the only answer, John 8:34

    c. assure Him of new life, 2 Cor. 5:17

3. Christians are so inconsistent

Do not try to argue against this charge. Admit it. There are hypocrites in the church, but there are many more outside than are inside the church.

    a. lack of understanding

    b. tell Him to turn his attention to himself

    c. show Him that every man will stand alone before God

    d. judging others is not a way of escaping judgment

4. We are all headed for heaven although along different roads

    a. sincerity does not mean salvation

    b. show Him what Jesus said, John 14:6, John 10:7

5. The Christian life is too hard

    a. Christian life is not behaviorism, but a new life, 2 Cor. 5:17

    b. we do not live the Christian life alone, Phil 4:13

6. God is too good to send sinners in hell[42]

---

[42] It is suggested that the reader please consider the following two articles:
Hellfire - Eternal Torment?
http://www.christianpublishers.org/hellfire-eternal-torment

a. God is good

b. God is just

c. God offered a way of salvation

d. it is only fair to send to hell those who rejected His love

Dr. R. A. Torrey preached a sermon entitled, "God's Blockade of the Road to Hell." In it he pointed out the many blockades God has put in a man's way to Hell. Some of them are: "The Bible," "The mother's prayers," "The mother's teaching and influence," "The sermons one heard," "The Holy Spirit and His work," "The Cross." If a man goes to hell it will be because he did not pay attention to the many blockades God has put in his way. The excuses will not do the unbeliever any good in the day of judgment, Matt. 25:31-46. As an evangelist, do not be offended by the unbeliever's excuses, be polite, depend on the Holy Spirit to give you the right answers to those excuses.

Evangelism and God's Sovereignty

There is real tension between the freedom of man and God's sovereignty. The truth that God is sovereign is clearly expressed in the Bible. He has sovereign control over all earthly affairs. He is the Lord of history and the Lord of the Christians' lives.

He has a perfect plan for everything that takes place in our universe, and nothing can thwart God's plan; all that occurs is in keeping with His will. On the other hand, the

Bible teaches the man is responsible for his actions, Genesis 2, 3. Gad gave Adam the "freedom" to do what he likes concerning the tree of the knowledge good and evil. God knew that Adam would sin, but His knowledge did not determine Adam to sin. In Evangelism, this tension is not easily solved. If God is in complete control of everything that moves in this world, than He can bring to Himself all those who are elected without any help from us. Yet in the New Testament we read the clear teaching of Jesus about evangelism. He gave a commission and He expects us to fulfill it.

There are some ultra-Calvinists that do not care about evangelism. They strongly believe in God's election, and as a result, they do not evangelize. Somehow, in His time God will take care of His elected to come to Him.

It is this the Bible teaching?

No, definitely no! In Acts 18:9-10 God's election functions as an incentive to evangelism not as a disincentive.

The idea is that if God has "His people" out there, then <u>the appropriate thing for Christians to do is to get involved in evangelism</u>, precisely because that is working with God and not against Him. Moreover, if God has His people there, Paul is assured of results, not because he is such a gifted evangelist, but because God's people will in a due course come to Him. Paul could have said, "If God has many people in this city, than I will go in another city to preach the gospel, those who are in this city will come to Jesus anyway." Still, instead of saying that, Paul determined to preach with all his power to reach those who are elected. God's sovereignty and His election do not stop evangelism, but gives motivation to proclaim the Good News to all men. We do

125

not know those who are elected to preach the Gospel only for them. We preach the Gospel, tell the Good News to all men in this way the elected can respond. The elected are in the world not knowing that they are elected. I did not know that I was elected until I heard the gospel, by the power of the Holy Spirit I responded, and when I was in, I saw on the back of the door, "**For He chose us in Him <u>before the creation of the world</u> to be holy and blameless in His sight**," Eph. 1:4. After I read that, I continued, "He predestined us to be adopted as his sons through Jesus Christ, according to **His pleasure and will**,"—Ephesians 1:5

Jesus said to go and preach the Gospel and He will take care of the results. He said that God would save those who will believe, but not those who will not believe, they are lost. This means that the elect will answer to the message, and those who are not elected will not. How God will judge them it is not our business, Romans 9:19-23. Our business is to get busy and tell everyone about the great salvation we received, because no one would come to Christ unless someone will tell them, Romans 10:14-17.

J. I. Packer in his book, "Evangelism and the Sovereignty of God" outlines the Biblical answer to the tension of evangelism and God's sovereignty, pages 96-122:

I. **The sovereignty of God in grace does not affect anything about the nature and the duty of evangelism.**

    a. the belief that God is sovereign in grace does not affect the <u>necessity</u> of evangelism

    b. the belief that God is sovereign in grace does not affect the <u>urgency</u> of evangelism

    c. the belief in God's sovereignty in grace does not affect the <u>genuineness</u> of the gospel invitation or the <u>truth</u> of the gospel promises

    d. the belief that God is sovereign in grace does not affect the <u>responsibility of the sinner</u> for his reaction to the Gospel; a man who rejects Christ becomes the cause of his own condemnation

II. **The sovereignty of God in grace gives our only hope of success in evangelism**

    a. this confidence makes us <u>bold</u>

    b. this confidence makes us <u>patient</u>

    c. this confidence makes us <u>prayerful</u>

Child Evangelism

They confronted the Lord Jesus Christ with a special situation in Matthew 19:13-15. Some mothers brought their children to Him. The Bible does not tell us if the mothers believed in Jesus as the Messiah, or not, but it is very interesting that those mothers wanted their children to be prayed over by that Man. The mothers had a great idea, but the disciples of Jesus were not too happy to see the Master stopping His teachings and blessed some "children." Yet Jesus is not too busy when children are around. Children have always been a high priority to God. Jesus does not need the protection against children, no; he needed protection from bumbling adults! "Do not hinder them!" "Let them come," Jesus said to the people around Him. Then He took time to touch the children, to pray over them, to bless them. What a Savior!

He had time for the little children, does the Church? Does the society? Someone said that "no society is smaller than the one that sees no obligation to its children."

Throughout the Bible, we can see that God was interested in children. He saved a little Moses and made Him the great leader of the Exodus. He called the little Samuel and made Him the greatest Judge of Israel. He found the young David and made Him the greatest king that Israel ever had. When Jeremiah was but a child, God called him to be the weeping prophet, and nobody wept more that him over the fate of Jerusalem. We read in 2 Kings 5 that God used a little girl to direct the Syrian general to Samaria to be cured of his leper. Children in the hands of God became great instruments for God's glory. Can a church or a society afford not to invest in its children? In fact without the children there is no future for neither church nor the society. Still, our society murders them, and murders them by the millions. What a shame!

Child Evangelism Fellowship is committed to let every child in America and hopefully, from around the world to have at least the opportunity to be confronted with an intelligent presentation of the Gospel of Jesus Christ. Nevertheless, it is the Child Evangelism Fellowship's call to do this? Where are the churches? Where are the Christians? Jesus told all of us, "Do not hinder them, but let them come to Me!"

1. We must evangelize children for they are the next generation.

2. We must evangelize children for they are wet cement.

3. Children must be evangelized for it is almost the easiest thing in the world to lead a child from five to 10 years of age to a definite acceptance of Christ, (R. A. Torrey).

4. We must evangelize children, because you do not save a child but a life. God saved many great men as children.

5. We must evangelize children because Satan wants them.

The Christians should evangelize their own children. Many Christians' homes have their children lost in the world. Why? They assumed that the Church or the Christian school will do the job. Both the Church and the Christian schools do the job of evangelizing the children, but the main responsibility rests on the family. In the Old Testament, we read about the obligation of the family to teach their children the laws of God, Deut. 6:7. They did not send their children to the Sunday School teacher to take care of their education, instead, they did the job.

Every father in Israel taught their children about God; in Psalm 78 we read: "I will open my mouth in parables, I will utter things hidden from the old--things we have heard and known, things our fathers have told us," vs. 2-3. There is no doubt where people got their knowledge. Their parents told them. The children of our times do not know hidden things, the things of God because their parents do not have time to tell them. The parents assume that the Church or the Christian school will take care of their religious education. Reading further in Psalm 78, we see what the evangelized children did, "we will not hide them from their children, we will tell the next generation." Why? For "He commanded our forefathers to teach their children, so the next generation would know them, even the children yet to be born. They in turn would tell their children," vs. 4-6.

The obligation of the parents is to tell their children about God and He will do the rest. Psalm 78:7 says, "Then they would put their trust in God, and would not forget His deeds."

In the New Testament we read about Timothy, the young preacher that Paul charged to do the work of an evangelist, how he knew the Scriptures from infancy from his mother and grandmother. They did not wait to see if Timothy is elected or not, if he likes the Scriptures or not, they taught him the Scriptures. God made Him a brave soldier of the Cross. Without knowing Timothy personally, we have to love this young man because Paul loved Him and trusted Him. Those two ladies taught Him the Scriptures, the Old Testament, and God arranged for Paul to meet Him and lead Him to Christ.

How to Lead a Child to Christ

Countless mothers and fathers led their children to Jesus Christ through their own method, and never wrote a book on how to lead a child to Christ. However, they have the joy of having their children along with them on the way to Heaven. Each of us can use another method, and no one could be wrong if we lead the children to Jesus. Paul does not tell us how he led Timothy to Christ, but we can assume that Eunice and Lois played a great role in that.

We can make the Gospel presentation simpler for children, but children must know that they are sinners, too. Some people give the impression that the children are not as "guilty" as the adult people are, and in one sense they are right. However, in many senses they are not. Children and adults are sinners not because they sinned, but because God imputed Adam's sin to all the humankind. Paul wrote in Romans 5:12-19 that sin entered the world through one man, and the result was that all men are considered sinners. Children must know that they need salvation as any adult does.

1. Tell the child that he or she needs salvation, Rom. 3:23.

2. Tell them that Jesus is the only Way of salvation, John 14:6.

3. Tell them that Jesus called the children to Him, Matt.19.

4. Tell the children that Jesus loves them

5. Tell them that they need to accept Jesus by faith

6. Help the child to pray and ask Jesus into his or her heart

7. Do not force a child into receiving Jesus; allow Him the freedom to say yes or no

Children must "see" the love of Christ in their parents or teachers. In child evangelism practicing the love of Christ is imperative. Children do not respond well to the "preaching" of nonpracticing parents. Children respond to love more than they do to preaching. I had the joy of kneeling down with my son and helped Him to invite Jesus into his heart. This is the ideal situation, the parent leading his children to Christ. Still, so many children without a family need Jesus too. The local church has to contact these children and invite them to their Sunday School. That will be a good starting point. Single parents will allow their children to the Sunday School, and often the children are converted, and then they can lead their parents to the Lord.

Another good method is the neighborhood children's Bible study. We can organize these groups almost everywhere. Children like to be together. They like company.

We can invite children from one block to your house for an evening of Bible stories, Bible videos, ice-cream. The leader should be warm and friendly. The videos or the stories should not be too long, but all must have some kind of challenge. Be sensitive to the individual needs. Allow time for decisions.

God converted Polycarp, the courageous early church martyr, when he was nine years old. Jonathan Edward, perhaps the mightiest intellect of the American pulpit, was saved at seven. Count Zinzerdorf, leader of the Moravians, was saved when he was four. Matthew Henry, the great commentator, was converted at 11, and Robert Hall, the great Baptist preacher, received Christ at 12.

A Word of Caution

Adults should never approach someone else's child, without the permission of their parents. Even then, no adult should ever be alone with one child. There are far too many child victims of adults taking advantage of them sexually. Moreover, false claims could be made, and one never recovers from false claims.

Evangelism Explosion

Reading the first chapters of the book of Acts and not noticing the "explosion" of evangelism, is impossible. Christ gave the disciples the command and the promise, to wait and receive power, and then to go and be His witnesses, (Acts 1:8). They waited, and in chapter two, we read that the Holy Spirit came and the "explosion" began. One of Peter's sermons brought 3,000 people to the point of asking, "Brothers, what shall we do?" These 3,000 were not from the two hundred churches of Jerusalem who attended the meeting and came to rededicate their lives, no, they were among those who shouted, "crucify Him, crucify Him!" That was "explosion." Nevertheless, the "explosion" did not stop there. The disciples, along with the 3,000 of new converts shared the Gospel with their friends, and in a few days they were 5,000! The Grace of God saved people, His great power healed the sick, the fear of God was present everywhere. They persecuted the apostles, but they continued to proclaim and pray. They stoned Stephen to death, they imprisoned Peter, but the church prayed. The results? "The Lord <u>added</u> to their number daily those who were being saved," Acts 2:47b. How was that "explosion" possible? What about today? Our world does need such an "explosion?" I believe it does. The problem is not with the world. The world is in the same situation that it was 2,000 years ago. Man needed salvation than and he needs it now. The problem is with the church, the Christians of our days.

The church in Acts expected God to work. The disciples waited for the Spirit to come, and when it came, they did not wait another minute, they started to proclaim Jesus.

Soon after I graduated from the Baptist Seminary in Bucharest, I went to help my father-in-law in the Baptist Church of Medias, Romania. It was the summer of 1980. The church was about 300 members, and it was a praying church. For many years, they prayed for revival. In the sixties, they experienced an "internal" revival, when most of the members rededicated their lives to Christ, and pledged to live a holy life. The years went by and they wanted an "outside" revival, when souls from that city would come to Christ. It came. On a specific Sunday, the church was ready for a baptismal service, with 19 new converts. During his message, my father-in-law gave an unusual invitation: "if someone here is ready to accept Jesus as his savior and Lord, and if he wants to be baptized, we will baptize Him today!" This was new. All the converts had to be prepared in a special way for baptismal, and he knew that. He was a Baptist preacher for more than 30 years but said it, and 38 people came forward. "Explosion!"

Everyone in the congregation was in awe, including him. I invited the new converts in the basement of the church, and while my co-pastor was baptizing the 19 "prepared" converts, I was preaching to the new ones. I was shaking. My voice trembled. I explained them what they did, I assured myself that they understood the message of the Gospel, and then I told them, "we are sorry. However, we cannot baptize you. We do not have enough white robes . . . " That was my idea but not theirs. I called the Pentecostal and the P.B. churches and asked them to send me their white robes. All they could produce were 10-15 . . . "See," I told them, "next week it will be another baptismal service, and we will baptize you then." One young man said, "What about the wet robes . . . ?" I was shocked. In my mind, I began to be sure that this is

134

of the Holy Spirit. These are not faking. They are genuine. We baptized them all. We baptized some robes twice that day! From that day in 1980 until the day we were forced to leave Romania in 1986, The Lord added to our number those whom He saved, more than 500 people.

Evangelism explosion is the demonstration of the Holy Spirit in bringing people to Christ through those who are available to Him. When the people of God make themselves available to the Holy Spirit, He will work through them.

Paul wrote to the Romans to bring their bodies as a living sacrifice, to renew their minds, and to not allow their lives to be modeled after the world's model, (Romans 12:1-2). Revival does not come without dedication. When the disciples received the Holy Spirit, the people could not ignore that demonstration of God's power. God was mightily at work in the Day of Pentecost. They could see and hear his activity in the lives of His people and felt. In Medias, after that baptismal service, God's power was real in transforming people. Members in the Communist Party gave up their membership; God changed husbands that abused their wives. God's power transformed drunkards in new people.

All that demonstration produced fascination. They asked the disciples about the meaning of the unusual event. God's demonstration always produces fascination, amazement, and wonder. More and more people in the city of Medias and all over Romania became fascinated with the work in our church. People came to the church and could not believe that their loved ones, their children, their friends were transformed. At one point, the secret police spread the rumor that in our church we kill children, and suck their blood. As a result, many children came to the services and brought their parents along. We did not know about their interests, but we preached the blood . . . the blood of Jesus that takes way our sins. They were fascinated, and many of them accepted Christ as their Savior.

However, after fascination came the explanation. Peter explained them what that demonstration real meant. He told them about Jesus' work of salvation, and reminded them about the promises of the Holy Spirit, the result, <u>Explosion!</u>

Acts two presents the <u>demonstration</u>, the <u>fascination</u>, the <u>explanation</u>, and the <u>explosion</u>, but the presentation does not stop there. To keep the "explosion," going, the believers: "devoted themselves to the apostles' teaching, and to the fellowship, to the breaking of the bread, and to prayer," (Acts 2:42). Study the Bible, keep the fellowship, take the Lord's Supper and pray, pray, pray!

The world is lost in sin. We need to act now. We are faced with a formidable task: world evangelization.

Every believer must make himself available to the Holy Spirit for the task of bringing others to Jesus Christ.

The Church's primary task is "every-member evangelism." The Church, having come to Christ, is to go for Christ. In our church of Medias, every member had one thing in their minds, "Medias for Christ." That was our goal, the whole city brought to the Cross. Every member had a prayer list; even the children had a prayer list that included all of the 70,000 people living then in our city, Medias. Our plan, our goal scared the communists; they feared us. They were afraid of our prayers. Authorities forced us to leave the city, but we continue to pray, and the work is going on. Everyone in that church not only prayed but also shared the Gospel with their friends. Bibles were not many. Tracts were not available. We did not have tapes. We knew the simple plan of salvation, and we knew our testimonies well. We counted on the Holy Spirit.

Dr. James Kennedy, of Coral Ridge Presbyterian Church in Fort Lauderdale, Florida, in his book "Evangelism Explosion," outlines how a whole congregation can be motivated and mobilized to do the task of evangelism. The pastor himself must provide the example and leadership in this task.

In the task of personal evangelism, the introduction may be the most difficult part of all. The way we approach the person we want to witness is important for the whole presentation.

Dr. Kennedy suggests this introduction:

A. Their secular life.

B. Their church life.

C. Our church.

D. Testimony: personal or church

E. Two Questions:

    1. Have you come to a place in your spiritual life where you know for certain if you were to die today you would go to heaven?

    2. Suppose that you were to die tonight and stand before God and he were to say to you, "Why should I let you into my heaven?" What would you say?

F. Transition

Your testimony can make the difference. Keep it brief, and make it provocative. If you do not have a testimony . . . you need one! You can use the testimony of your church.

After you earned the right to continue, proceed immediately into the Gospel:

A. GRACE

    1. Eternal life, a home in heaven forever, a gift of God

    2. Eternal life is not deserved and cannot be earned

    3. Transition: This can be seen more clearly, when we see what the Bible says about <u>man and sin</u>

B. MAN

    1. Man is a sinner whose destiny is eternal hell

    2. Man cannot save himself

    3. Transition: The problem of man trying to save himself comes into sharper focus when we see what the Bible says about God

C. GOD

    1. God is infinitely holy and just and must punish sinners

    2. God is infinitely merciful and desires to pardon sinners

    3. Transition: God solved this apparent conflict by coming into this world in the person of Jesus Christ

D. JESUS CHRIST

1. Jesus Christ is the infinite God-Man

2. Jesus died to pay the penalty of our sins and arouse bodily from the dead and is alive today in heaven and intercedes for sinners. He offers eternal life as a free gift of God's grace.

3. Transition: This gift can be received only by faith.

What is faith?

E. FAITH

1. Faith is not mere intellectual assent nor temporal faith

2. Faith IS complete trust in Jesus Christ alone for forgiveness of sins and the gift of eternal life

3. Transition: Does this make sense to you?

If the answer is "No, it does not," find out what is not clear and seek to clarify it. Be patient. Remember when somebody else tried to present the Gospel to you!

If the answer is "Yes, it does," help the person if he wants to receive God's gift of eternal life, by putting his faith in the Lord Jesus Christ? If the answer is "No," do not try to "high pressure the person." On the other hand, "do not give up too easily," remember the adversary. Be sensitive. Know the difference.

If the answer is "yes," explain Him what decision he is going to take, the most important decision of his life. Explain that he receives God's gift by faith, and he recognizes himself as a sinner unable to save himself, but he trusts Christ alone for salvation. Yet Christ is not only Savior. He wants to be the Lord of his life. He must give Christ control of his life the best he knows. If the person does not understand, or does not want this, perhaps a second visit would be wise at this point. If he understands, and wants to receive God's gift, help Him to pray. Pray with Him, use short phrases, and be specific in your prayer. If he prayed, help Him to read at least two Bible verses, John 6:47, and Romans 10:13. Stick with these verses until the person confesses that he is saved by relying on what God says in His Word.

After the person received Christ, arrange with him for a chance to meet again, in a week or so to talk again about his decision. Assure him that you will continue to pray for Him. Encourage Him to read the Bible and to pray.

CHAPTER 10 The Importance of the Follow Up Ministry

On the same level important with the introduction and the gospel presentation, we find the follow-up ministry. Most recently, in Romania, after big evangelistic crusades conducted by Luis Palau, and other gifted evangelists, those who accepted Christ were in the thousands. Nevertheless, the real number of converts in Romania is still very small. Why? Besides other factors, a very important one is the total absence of the follow-up ministry. The people listened to the message, accepted it, but nobody follow-up their decision. That is a big mistake on the Christians' part. In a big campaign, with a good evangelist, they accepted Christ, but that is only the beginning. Much more must be done.

The Day of Pentecost ended with a church numbering more than 3,000 members. Great?! What about those disciples? For the last three years and a half, Jesus took care of their needs, physical and spiritual needs. Now they have to take care of more than 3,000!

How did they manage it?

Acts 2:42 tells us that they "devoted themselves to the apostles' teaching and to the fellowship, to the breaking of the bread and to prayer." This is how. They trained their converts.

Jesus in His great Commission said, "go and make disciples of all nations, baptizing them in the name of the father, and of the Son and of the Holy Spirit, and <u>teach them to obey everything I have commanded you</u>," Matt. 28:19-20.

After you led them to the Lord, you have to teach them the way they have to follow.

1. If we do not follow up the new believer, the devil will.

2. Salvation is merely the first step in the Christian life.

3. Persistence and personal attention are two key factors.

4. Worship and service should follow salvation.

Follow-up can be divided into two parts:

a. immediate follow-up

b. extended follow-up

The immediate follow-up implies:

a. a spiritual birthday, congratulations, recording the event

b. facts of life, church, a public profession, questions, Bible

c. definite invitation to church services

The extended follow-up takes two or more visits:

a. phone call before Sunday

b. a letter from the church

c. first follow-up visits

   1. review salvation, the two questions

   2. Bible study

   3. answer any eventual questions

   4. make appointment for second follow-up visits

    d. second follow-up visits

        1. try to be a friend without encroaching on his privacy

        2. Bible study

        3. use common sense in scheduling additional visits

    e. eventual pastoral visit

    f. further visits by other church people

    g. discipleship begins

Disciples are Made not Born

"Go and **make disciples** . . . "

This is what Jesus expects, not just "converts," but disciples, people to follow Him and learn from Him. After the "follow-up" visits, every new convert should be placed in a local church, and the process of becoming like Jesus begins. It is a long process, in fact, a lifelong process, and we all are striving to become "like Him." Although it is next to impossible, we have the hope that when we will see Him, "we will be like Him," 1 John 3:2. Yet until then, we must help any new convert to grow in grace, to become a mature Christian.

EVERY CHRISTIAN IS A DISCIPLE, BUT NOT EVERY DISCIPLE IS A CHRISTIAN!

What is a mature Christian?

1. A mature Christian knows that he is the child of God, grace saved him, 1 John 3:1; Eph. 2:8-9. Although doubt will visit anyone, mature Christians will be sure of their salvation, Rom. 8:1, 33-39. A new convert must be brought to the

point to be sure that what he did (asking Jesus into his heart), has eternal consequences, and nothing can separate Him from God.

Bible study and prayer are essential at this point, for in the Bible, we find our assurance, and by prayer we acknowledge that we trust in God for this assurance. Assurance is not in feelings, nor in somebody's experience, only in the Bible. A mature Christian can help a new convert to grow to his level of certainty concerning his or her salvation.

2. A mature Christian loves the fellowship of the other believers. In the book of Acts, we see that the disciples with the new converts loved to be together, to study the Word, to pray, and have the Lord's Supper, Acts 2:42. Immature believers avoid fellowship, sometimes looking for the "old fellowship," so we must train the new convert in this respect. Hebrews 10:25 tell us not to abandon the fellowship of the believers.

3. Mature believers are filled with the Holy Spirit, or they are under the Holy Spirit's control, Eph. 5:18. At the new birth, the Holy Spirit baptized every convert into the Body of Christ, 1 Cor. 12:13. That event was a judicial transaction, non-experimental, without our active participation. Being filled with the Holy Spirit means that we give the Holy Spirit total control in our lives, and this process takes the entire Christian life.

4. False doctrines, Eph. 4:14 do not move Mature Christians. Paul says, "do not be immature, or children," meaning that any wind of false doctrine can easily toss children.

A disciple making Christian will instruct any new convert to grow so that his spiritual feet will be well established in the Word of God.

5. A mature Christian can teach others, Heb. 4:12; 1 Tim. 3:2b. Jesus instructed his disciples for more than three years, and after that period, they started their ministry of teaching others. Although we are in the process of becoming more like Jesus, eventually, we must be able to "make disciples." Remember, it is the Holy Spirit who brings us to perfection.

6. Christians that are mature are heavenly minded, Col. 3:1-2. The world is not our home, we are going to live fore ever in Jesus' land, and as we grow in Christ, our minds are more fixed on the things that are there not here.

There are many more things that we should "teach" the new converts, but I believe that part of the church mission's is to continually teach its members "all that Christ commanded."

Spiritual Development

2 Peter 3:18: "Grow in grace and knowledge of our Lord and Savior Jesus Christ. To Him be the glory, both now and to the day of eternity."

2 Peter 1:3: "His divine power has granted to us everything concerning life and godliness through the true knowledge of Him."

There is a clear indication in these verses that we have to grow, to develop in our spiritual journey. New converts have to be "disciplined" through the initial steps of this lifelong journey. The Holy Spirit gave us all that we need pertaining to the natural life and the spiritual life. We have all our needs met in Him, Phil 4:19.

Ephesians 4:15 tells us to "grow up in all aspects into Him, who is the head, even Christ." Our spiritual development has to be in Christ, because we are born from above, and we are "live no longer, but Christ lives in us," Gal. 2:20.

A mature believer, a "discipler" will help the new believers to grasp these great truths about the spiritual development.

The Book of Acts gives us the apostles' model of discipleship, model that is still the best!

Acts 2:42: "And they were continually devoting themselves to the apostles' teaching and to fellowship, to the breaking of the bread, and to prayer."

1. The Apostle's Teaching

They introduced the new converts to Christianity to the "apostles' teaching." Although the book does not explain what these teachings were, we can safely assume that the disciples taught them what Jesus told them, Matt. 28:20. Those converts knew the Old Testament (they were Jews), but in today's world Bible knowledge is at a very low level (even among Christians!).

The Bible is vital in our spiritual development. It gives us life, James 1:18, and sustains our spiritual lives. It is the spiritual food for our spiritual growth, 1 Peter 2:2. A believer has to become very disciplined in studying the Word. There are many Bible reading plans available, but the best is that one that you can stick with and study systematically and consistently the Word of God!

2. Fellowship

We have reduced Today's Christianity fellowship to the coffee and the donuts in the 'fellowship' hall! The biblical "koinonia" means much more than that. The fellowship of the body is the mutual care and concern its members have for each other. Fellowship takes place when Christians come together to minister to one another in the power of the Holy Spirit. As members of the same body, we have to love one another, 1 Pet. 1:22; 1 John 4:7, 11; pray for one another, James 5:16; build up one another, 1 Thess. 5:11; bear one another's burdens, Gal. 6:2; serve one another, Gal. 5:13; be kind to one another, Eph. 5:21; restore one another, forgive one another; Gal. 6:1; Col. 3:13. These things are not common among the unsaved, but they have to grow in God's family. Peter says to "apply all diligence, in your faith supply moral excellence, and in your moral excellence, knowledge, and in your knowledge self- control, and in your self-control perseverance, and in your perseverance godliness, and your godliness, brotherly kindness, and your brotherly kindness, Christian love," 2 Pet. 1:5-7.

3. The Lord's Supper. Observing the Lord's Supper is very important for every believer. Jesus began this memorial before His arrest, and the disciples practiced it from the beginning. Paul instructs the Corinthian church to be very careful how they celebrate the Lord's Supper, 1 Cor. 11:23-34.

The New Testament church has only two symbols, baptism and the Lord's Supper, and learning to obey God's commandments is imperative for every new believer. Sitting is wise for the discipler next to the new believer when attending Lord's Supper for the first time.

3. Prayer

There is no spiritual development without prayer. There is not spiritual life without prayer. Jesus prayed while He was on this earth; the first Christians prayed; Paul prayed, and throughout the Church's history, millions and millions of Christians prayed. New Christians should be encouraged to pray immediately after they received Christ as their Savior. Simple expressing what they understand, what they do not understand, their needs and feelings will be a good start.

A Life of Discipline

Paul wrote to the young Timothy, "discipline yourself for the purpose of godliness," 1 Tim 4:7. We are saved by grace, but to be useful in God's kingdom we must live disciplined lives.

The purpose of the Christian life is to become like Jesus, growing from the "elementary things" to the maturity in Christ.

Jesus called us to take His yoke upon ourselves and learn from Himself, Matt 11:28-29. His life was a very disciplined life, a life that glorified God in every aspect.

The disciplines for the spiritual life are activities undertaken to bring us into more effective cooperation with Christ and His Kingdom. They are a means to accessing God's grace, because they made us capable of receiving more of His life and power that are given to us as a gift.

In the disciplines of abstinence, we abstain to some degree and for some time from the satisfaction of what we generally regard as legitimate desires. The disciplines of abstinence are:

1. Solitude: Purposefully abstaining from interaction with other human beings, denying ourselves companionship and all that comes from our conscious interaction with others. Jesus spent many days and many hours alone with God. While His disciples were traveling, or debating, He was in the mountains alone.

2. Silence: Closing off our souls from "sounds," noise, music, or words.

3. Fasting: Abstaining in some significant way from food and possible from drink as well.

4. Frugality: Abstaining from using money or goods at our disposal in ways that merely gratify our desires or our hunger for status, glamour, or luxury.

5. Chastity: Purposefully turning away from dwelling upon or engaging in the sexual dimension of our relationships to others even our husbands or wives.

6. Secrecy: Abstaining from causing our good deeds and qualities to be known.

7. Sacrifice: Abstaining from the possession or enjoyment of what is necessary for our living; forsaking the security of meeting our needs with what is in our hands; total abandonment of God, in the faith and hope that God will bear us up.

In the disciplines of engagement, we involve ourselves in actions that will help us grow and develop. The disciplines of engagement are:

1. Study: Engaging ourselves in the written and spoken Word of God.

2. Worship: Engaging ourselves in dwelling upon and expressing the greatness, beauty, and goodness of God through thought and the use of words, rituals, and symbols.

3. Celebration: Enjoying ourselves, our life, and our world in conjunction with our faith and confidence in God's greatness, beauty, and goodness.

4. Service: Engaging our goods and strength in the active promotion of the food and others and the causes of God in our world.

5. Prayer: Conversing, communicating with God.

6. Fellowship. Engaging in common activities of worship, study, prayer, celebration, and service with other disciples.

7. Confession: Letting trusted others know our deepest weaknesses and failures.

8. Submission: The highest level of fellowship involving humility, complete honesty, transparency, and at times confession and restitution.

The word "Christian" is found only three times in the New Testament, while the word "disciple" is found 269 times!

Are we Christians and disciples or only Christians?[43]

---

[43] Dallas Willard "The Spirit of the Disciplines."

APPENDIX A Teaching Our Children

Edward D. Andrews

Certainly, Christian parents would agree that teaching children is no easy task. However, this is the most important aspect of our Great Commission as parents. Our most important students are our children. Therefore, when our children freely choose God, it makes the time and effort worthwhile.

Psalm 78:7 New American Standard Bible (NASB)

⁷ That they should put their confidence in God
And not forget the works of God,
But keep His commandments,

What all is involved in effectively teaching our children? First, it is buying out the time for a family Bible study. This means that at least one day a week, the family gets together, husband and wife,[44] with children for a one-hour family Bible study. Second, you need to be consistent, so the children know that the parents are not indecisive in their commitment to the family study. Children these days have numerous timewasters: friends, cellphones, internet, television, games, and so on. The parents have to help the children realize, early on, the family study and their relationship with God has the greatest priority. In other words, there are no distractions at the family study, like a cellphone. All technology and friends are to be set aside for a half hour before, during and a half hour after the family study.

---

[44] If yours is a single parent family; then, the responsibility falls to the single parent.

The parents should work to make the family study as enjoyable as possible. The half hour before can be a time to sit, eat snacks, and find out how each person's week went. The half hour after the study can be for idle chitchat. This is to be a comfortable, stress-free time for learning. It should not be some formal, rigid study that is dreaded by the children. This can be done by having this night also include a special mealtime, like ordering pizza, or going out to eat after the study, even occasionally taking in a movie after the evening meal.

What should be studied at the family study? It could be a book, which everyone studies together. Alternatively, it could be the family preparing for a regular Christian meeting that they attend, which will instill in the children the need to be prepared for meetings. Whichever, it should be designed so that the children have a very active role in the study, nit simply reading to them. There needs to be questions and answers, giving them an opportunity to talk about the Bible in their own words. This will enable the children to feel comfortable discussing God's Word outside of Christian meetings.

The study should of course cover things that can be beneficial for the growth of the children. You may set aside fifteen minutes of each study to cover Bible topics that deal with being a teenager. This would include such things as peer pressure, bullying, dating, drugs, loneliness, gossip, self-control, and so on. Covering these, can help the young ones see that the Bible has practical answers, helping us walk with God even in this modern world that we live. This will embed biblical principles in the hearts of our children, so deeply that it will be their guiding force when we are not around. The only barrier is creating this free zone, so our children feel comfortable opening up to us. They need to know that their openness is rewarded with love, and that they can talk about anything that is on their young mind, without repercussions of shocked expressions, startled response, raised voices. They need to feel our love, knowing that we are deeply interested in them, and that we will be with them, supporting them through everything that young ones face these days.

It may be that we have children of different ages, like one that is six, and the other, who is fifteen. This would have to be considered, because they would not be on the same level, as far as taking in knowledge. It may be that the family study, in such a case as this, is set up so all can understand, with teenager playing a role of helping the young one get the points that are being made. Then, at the end, the teenager is given special attention by one parent, while the other parent is helping the young one. This should be alternated between parents, so both parents are drawing close to both children spiritually.

We as parents do not want to have unrealistic expectations, as there will be times that our children will have a low level of interest. They are no different from us, as the pressures of Satan's world will weigh them down as well, meaning that they may be moody at times, or uninterested. We need to pay attention to the length of such periods, and the depth of them. It is to be expected that the moods will appear occasionally, but if a child is moody or uninterested for a couple weeks straight; then, more is going on than a momentary feeling of unhappiness. If it is a teenage girl, the mother may take her out on another occasion, to see if she can get her to confide in her. If it is a teenage boy, the father may do the same.

The father is to take serious his role as the head of the family. If the mother is a single parent; then, she is responsible for the spirituality of the children. Regardless, the challenge of teaching the children belongs to us, and we need to take it seriously. Nevertheless, if you are the child, depending on your age, you are accountable to God, to contribute toward your parent's role in the family study, by participating fully. Each of us has been given the special gift of life, and the hope of eternal life, for which we should truly appreciate our heavenly Father.

Prayer for Spiritual Power

Ephesians 3:14-19 Holman Christian Standard Bible (HCSB)

[14] For this reason I kneel before the Father [15] from whom every family in heaven and on earth is named. [16] I pray that He may grant you, according to the riches of His glory, to be strengthened with power in the inner man through His Spirit, [17] and that the Messiah may dwell in your hearts through faith. I pray that you, being rooted and firmly established in love,[18] may be able to comprehend with all the saints what is the length and width, height and depth of God's love, [19] and to know the Messiah's love that surpasses knowledge, so you may be filled with all the fullness of God.

APPENDIX B The Field is the World

Edward D. Andrews

Matthew 13:37-39 English Standard Version (ESV)

³⁷ He answered, "The one who sows the good seed is the Son of Man. ³⁸ The field is the world, and the good seed is the sons of the kingdom. The weeds are the sons of the evil one, ³⁹ and the enemy who sowed them is the devil. The harvest is the end of the age, and the reapers are angels.

Here Jesus is explaining his parable of the *wheat and the weeds*. Here Jesus says that he is "the one who sows the good seed," the Son of Man. However, it is clear that Christians are doing the work for Jesus, as they go about sowing the Word of God. The "field" is the world of humankind, who are alienated from God, and need to be cultivated [reasoned with], as Christians go about sowing the good seed [evangelization] of biblical truth. This field encompasses the whole world.

Each Christian has their own part of that "field" to evangelize, which would be their local community. Have you been going about sowing the Word of God in your community? Does your church go out into their community sowing the good seed [evangelization] of biblical truth? More specifically, are you carrying out the command of Christ, to carry out the Great Commission. (Matthew 28:19-20) How do you feel about the community that you live within? Do you view them as a community of souls that need saved? Are they not living souls who have their personal affections, despairs, needs, distresses and necessities, and who may very well take to the path of life, as opposed to the path of destruction? How are they to hear the Word of God, unless you take it to them?

Romans 10:14-15 English Standard Version (ESV)

¹⁴ How then will they call on him in whom they have not believed? And how are they to believe in him of whom they have never heard? And how are they to hear without someone preaching? ¹⁵ And how are they to preach unless they are sent? As it is written, "How beautiful are the feet of those who preach the good news!"

Do you see them a potential future spiritual brother or sister, ones made originally in God's image and likeness, People whom God so loved that he gave his only Son, that whoever believes in him should not perish but have eternal life. (John 3:16) Should we not view your community the same way that God would view it? Let us take a short trip to an ancient biblical city, one we would not expect to be show mercy.

The Bloody City of Nineveh

Nahum 3:1 English Standard Version (ESV)

¹ Woe to the bloody city, all full of lies and plunder, no end to the prey!

Image 1 Ancient City of Nineveh

Nahum delivers the prophetic decree upon Nineveh, the capital of Assyria, the second world power of Bible history, the queen city of the earth at the time. Assyria was like a pack of lions on the hunt, as they were feared by all in the then known earth. Viciousness and inhumanity held sway in the supreme. It is by warfare that Nineveh enriched itself, becoming the greatest and most feared city of the day.

Genesis 10:9-12 English Standard Version (ESV)

⁹He was a **mighty hunter before Jehovah**: wherefore it is said, Like Nimrod a mighty hunter before Jehovah. ¹⁰And the beginning of his kingdom was Babel, and Erech, and Accad, and Calneh, in the land of Shinar. ¹¹Out of that land he went forth into Assyria, and builded Nineveh, and Rehoboth-ir, and Calah, ¹²and Resen between Nineveh and Calah (the same is the great city).

The cruel and ruthless Nimrod was the cities founder; thus, it is hardly surprising that the life in the day of Nineveh would be filled with bloodshed and cruelty. Nimrod was renowned as a "mighty hunter 'before'" (in a negative and hostile sense; Heb., liphneh; "against" or "in opposition to"; compare Nu 16:2; 1Ch 14:8; 2Ch 14:10) or "in front of" Jehovah. It is true that some scholars view the Hebrew preposition in a favorable sense, meaning "in front of;" however, the Jewish Targums, the first-century Jewish historian Josephus, as well as the context of Genesis chapter 10 paints a different picture of Nimrod, as a hunter in rebelliousness toward Jehovah.

If the suburbs of Calah and Resen were being considered, Nineveh made up one great city. It was for its great wickedness that Jehovah God sent Jonah the prophet to Nineveh. It was only by the Ninevites' repentant attitude that they avoided be destroyed by God. However, it was not long that this great city and its inhabitants fell back into their former wicked ways. Throughout the period of influence of Kings Sargon, Sennacherib, Esar-haddon and Ashurbanipal, Nineveh stretched out to the height of its wickedness and bloody undertakings. Ashurnasirpal, describes his punishment of several rebellious cities in this way,

> "I built a pillar over against his city gate, and I flayed all the chief men who had revolted, and I covered the pillar with their skins; some I walled up within the pillar, some I impaled upon the pillar on stakes, ... and I cut off the limbs of the officers, of the royal officers who had rebelled. ... Many captives from among them I burned with fire, and many I took as living captives. From some I cut off their hands and their fingers, and from others I cut off their noses, their ears, and their fingers(?), of many I put out the eyes. I made one pillar of the living, and another of heads, and I bound their heads to posts (tree trunks) round about the city. Their young men and maidens I burned in the fire ... Twenty men I captured alive and I immured them in the wall of his palace. ... The rest of them [their warriors] I consumed with thirst in the desert of the Euphrates."[45]

As the Assyrian army arrived back to Nineveh from a successful campaign, its captives were well aware of the horrors that awaited them, for they were in for unthinkable suffering and cruelty. As the soldiers came over the horizon,

---

[45] *Ancient Records of Assyria and Babylonia*, by D. D. Luckenbill, 1926, Vol. I, pp. 145, 147, 153, 162.

there would be an numerous line of captives, being led by cords that had hooks, which were pierced through the nose or lips. Many could look forward to being blinded by the King of Nineveh himself, who would use the point of a spear. Other prisoners awaited impalement, being hanged by their nude bodies upon pointed stakes that were run up through the stomachs into the chest cavities of the victims. Others still, were whipped or beaten severely and then had their skin removed from their body while still alive. It is this fear factor that made Nineveh the great military machine that would march on another city, and its inhabitants would surrender without a fight.

Nahum 2:9 English Standard Version (ESV)

⁹ Plunder the silver, plunder the gold! There is no end of the treasure or of the wealth of all precious things.

The campaigns of war were very profitable to the merchants of Nineveh, who were as numerous as the sands of the sea, or so it must have seemed. Wealth like a river during flood season, poured into the great city. The shops throughout were filled with the most precious luxurious items and appliances that the then known world had to offer. What treasures fill this ancient city!

Regardless of Nineveh's cruelty and viciousness, it was exceptionally religious. *Unger's Bible Dictionary* (1965, p. 102) states: "These gods are invoked at times severally in phrases which seem to raise each in turn to a position of supremacy over the others." Notice to the number of deities revealed in this section from the *Annals of Ashurbanipal*: "By the command of Ashur, Sin, Shamash, Ramman, Bel, Nabu, Ishtar of Nineveh, Ninib, Nergal, and Nusku, I entered the land of Mannai and marched through it victoriously. Its cities, great and small, which were without number, as far as Izirtu, I captured, I destroyed, I devastated, I burned with fire."

The priests of Nineveh were not against war; to the contrary, they were supports of the nation's primary source of income. In fact, they were largely the cause, stirring up trouble that would lead to war. This may not seem so surprising, when one learns that their livelihood is supported by the conquest of war, as they would get their customary percentage before any other party. The reason for such is the ultra-religious society of the people, believing it was the gods, who gave them victory. Those greedy priests were thrilled at the sight of the beginnings of a war campaign, and the return of the military with its spoils.

Returning from our trip to ancient Nineveh, we can certainly gain a feeling of how God would view your community, especially once we hear the words he uttered to Jonah his prophet,

Jonah was commissioned to preach to Nineveh, but he chose to run away:

Jonah 1:1-2 American Standard Version (ASV)

1 Now the word of Jehovah came unto Jonah the son of Amittai, saying, ² "Arise, go to Nineveh, that great city, and cry against it; for their wickedness is come up before me." ³ But Jonah rose up to flee unto Tarshish from the presence of Jehovah; and he went down to Joppa, and found a ship going to Tarshish: so he paid the fare thereof, and went down into it, to go with them unto Tarshish from the presence of Jehovah

God repeats his command to Jonah. However, this times Jonah does not evade the commission he was given, so he goes to Nineveh.

Jonah 3:4 English Standard Version (ESV)

⁴ Jonah began to go into the city, going a day's journey. And he called out, "Yet forty days, and Nineveh shall be overthrown!"

The city of Nineveh repents,

Jonah 3:5 English Standard Version (ESV)

⁵ And the people of Nineveh believed God. They called for a fast and put on sackcloth, from the greatest of them to the least of them.

Their repentance saved them in that day,

Jonah 3:10 English Standard Version (ESV)

¹⁰ When God saw what they did, how they turned from their evil way, God relented of the disaster that he had said he would do to them, and he did not do it.

Jonah did not receive this great act of mercy well; it was more than he could take,

Jonah 4 Updated American Standard Version (UASV)

¹ But it displeased Jonah exceedingly, and he was angry. ² And he prayed to Jehovah, and said, "O Jehovah, was not this what I said while I was still in my *own* country? Therefore I made haste to flee to Tarshish; for I knew that you are a gracious God, and merciful, slow to anger, and abundant in loving kindness, and one who relents concerning calamity. ³ Therefore now, O Jehovah, please take my life from me, for it is better for me to die than to live."

Now, the reader of this historical account is introduced to just how those characteristics of God that Jonah uttered above, relate to his feelings for the city of Blood, Nineveh,

Jonah 4:11 English Standard Version (ESV)

¹¹ "And should not I pity Nineveh, that great city, in which there are more than 120,000 persons who do not know their right hand from their left, and also much cattle?"

One Bible scholar offers us these insights,

> [Jonah] 4:10. God tried to calm his prophet with a bit of simple reasoning. Let's compare your situation with my situation. You watched a vine get eaten away and got all worked up with concern and pity over the vine. Now this vine was something that just came to you. "You did not labor over it, and you did not make it grow. It appeared one night, and it was destroyed in one night" (Literally, "which was the son of a night and perished the son of a night"). Think about the real value of this vine. "Does my prophet love a one-day-wonder-gourd vine more than my eternal mission?"
>
> [Jonah] 4:11. "That's your situation, Jonah. Now look at mine. If you love the vine that much, can't I love Nineveh at least that much? Look at all the poor, innocent, ignorant people! Love them with me. Or love your prejudice. Which will it be?"[46]

---

[46] Anders, Max; Butler, Trent (2005-10-01). *Holman Old Testament Commentary - Hosea, Joel, Amos, Obadiah, Jonah, Micah* (Kindle Locations 7132-7138). B&H Publishing. Kindle Edition.

Can you imagine the indifference, rejection, opposition, and threats on his life that Jonah must have encountered as he spent days walking through the most evil city on earth. This is some of what Christians would face as well, if they were to enter into their communities around the world. However, are the people not "persons who do not know their right hand from their left, and also much cattle?" (4:11) Nevertheless, we are looking for those with a receptive heart, which may very well be one in a hundred, maybe one in a thousand. Our task is to cultivate the ground by reasoning from the Scriptures, as we sow the seed of the Word of God. However, it is God, who will make that seed grow, if the person has a receptive heart.

1 Corinthians 3:5-9 English Standard Version (ESV)

⁵ What then is Apollos? What is Paul? Servants through whom you believed, as the Lord assigned to each. ⁶ I planted, Apollos watered, but God gave the growth. ⁷ So neither he who plants nor he who waters is anything, but only God who gives the growth. ⁸ He who plants and he who waters are one, and each will receive his wages according to his labor. ⁹ For we are God's fellow workers. You are God's field, God's building.

Yes, millions of churches are not even entering into their community to carry out the work they have been assigned. If they were to do so, they would find that God will help open the hearts of the sheep like ones, who will then pay attention to the Word.

Acts 16:14 English Standard Version (ESV)

¹⁴ One who heard us was a woman named Lydia, from the city of Thyatira, a seller of purple goods, who was a

worshiper of God. The Lord opened her heart to pay attention to what was said by Paul.

The churches that are failing to fulfill the Great Commission, lack the proper motive, the proper Christian spirit, which the people of their community never get to hear. There are even those who would oppose such evangelism, but over time may soften to the Christian message in these difficult times.

If you are reading this article, and your heart is rushing at the thought that you have never being given the chance to evangelize your community, because your church never trained you for such, do not give up hope. However, never allow anyone, even a pastor to offer reasons as to why this work is not being done in your community, or being done in a different way. You need to show persistence, real seriousness and concern in people by proclaiming the Word of God to them. This brings us back to Paul's question to the Roman Christians.

Romans 10:14-15 English Standard Version (ESV)

¹⁴ How then will they call on him in whom they have not believed? And how are they to believe in him of whom they have never heard? And how are they to hear without someone preaching? ¹⁵ And how are they to preach unless they are sent? As it is written, "How beautiful are the feet of those who preach the good news!"

You can just as easily send yourself, and other likeminded Christians, by taking it upon yourself. The Evangelism Handbook: How All Christians Can Effectively Share God's Word in Their Community by Andrews, Edward D. (Aug 28, 2013)[47]

---

[47] http://www.christianpublishers.org/apps/webstore/products/show/4676258

APPENDIX C Evangelizing with a Spirit of Willingness

Edward D. Andrews

God's people willing offer themselves to their heavenly Father just before the return of Jesus Christ.

Psalm 110:3 Updated American Standard Version (UASV)

³ Your people will offer themselves willingly
   on the day of your power,
   in holy array;
from the womb of the dawn,
   the dew of Your youth belongs to you.

Our heavenly Father and his Son, Jesus Christ will be well pleased with those who offer themselves willingly, evangelizing with their whole soul, mind, heart and spirit.

2 Corinthians 9:7 English Standard Version (ESV)

⁷ Each one must give as he has decided in his heart, not reluctantly or under compulsion, for God loves a cheerful giver.

If God loves a cheerful giver, one that is not under compulsion, or reluctant, why did Paul say in his previous letter to the Corinthians, "For if I preach the gospel, that gives me no ground for boasting. For necessity is laid upon me. Woe to me if I do not preach the gospel!" Here Paul is saying, "Necessity is laid upon" him, and 'Woe to me if I do not preach the gospel!' Which is it? On the other hand, did Paul change his mind in the few months between First and Second Corinthians? It is not a contradiction, or change of mind, as they both agree. A necessity is laid upon us, but God wants us to do it willingly, not under compulsion. The "woe" that Paul felt was not out of some fear of reprisal, if he did not carry out his ministry of evangelism. Rather, it was a feeling of "woe," because he felt the same as God, the love for the people fear that they would miss the hope of "life." Paul was well aware of and empathetic to the Hebrew Old Testament texts, such as

Ezekiel 3:18 English Standard Version (ESV)

[18] If I say to the wicked, 'You shall surely die,' and you give him no warning, nor speak to warn the wicked from his wicked way, in order to save his life, that wicked person shall die for his iniquity, but his blood I will require at your hand.

Warning the Wicked

It is our responsibility to give a warning to the wicked people, just as it was Ezekiel's responsibility to give a warning to Judah. Ezekiel, Paul and us realize that God's love for humanity, who suffers from imperfection and the desire to do wicked things; need to be warned as well. Yes, Paul loved the people he witnessed to, and so should we. If we go ahead and look at the next verse, we will see that Paul willingly carried out his ministry, making personal sacrifice in order to do so.

1 Corinthians 9:17 English Standard Version (ESV)

[17] For if I do this of my own will, I have a reward, but if not of my own will, I am still entrusted with a stewardship.

It should sadden all of us that so many out of so-called conservative Christianity are not arranging their lives around an evangelism program, because their church is not carrying out the work. Nevertheless, this series of books on evangelism cannot judge the hearts its readers. However, Paul himself clearly said, "each one tests his own work, and then his reason to boast will be in himself alone and not in his neighbor." (Gal. 6:4) We are well aware of the fact that many of us have families, and Paul was quite clear about our need to care for them too. He wrote, "But if anyone does not provide for his relatives, and especially for members of his household, he has denied the faith and is worse than an unbeliever." (1 Tim. 5:8) Regardless, our love of our neighbor and even our enemy (Matt. 5:43-44), should move us to have some share in the evangelism work, we simply need to buy out the time. If our church has nothing along these lines, we may want to inquire as to why.

Hebrews 4:12 English Standard Version (ESV)

12 For the word of God is living and active, sharper than any two-edged sword, piercing to the division of soul and of spirit, of joints and of marrow, and discerning the thoughts and intentions of the heart.

When we take the time to look at ourselves through the lenses of the Scriptures, it will enable us to see the intentions of our heart. Therefore, it is imperative that we read some of God's Word daily, as well as have a daily personal study of God's Word. As we study, we need to meditate on what God is saying to us through his Word, so we will have what he thinks and feels not what we think and feel. Even more so, over time we will develop the mind of Christ, so that our thoughts and feelings will be biblical, i.e., the thoughts of God.

2 Peter 1:5-8 English Standard Version (ESV)

⁵ For this very reason, make every effort to supplement your faith with virtue, and virtue with knowledge, ⁶ and knowledge with self-control, and self-control with steadfastness, and steadfastness with godliness, ⁷ and godliness with brotherly affection, and brotherly affection with love. ⁸ For if these qualities are yours and are increasing, they **keep you from being ineffective or unfruitful** in the knowledge of our Lord Jesus Christ.

If we supply the above to our faith, Peter says, they [will] **keep you from being ineffective or unfruitful**. (2 Pet. 1:8) On the other hand, Peter says,

2 Peter 1:9 English Standard Version (ESV)

⁹ For whoever lacks these qualities is so nearsighted that he is blind, having forgotten that he was cleansed from his former sins.

If these proper qualities and activities were missing from our lives, we would have something for which we should be very concerned. If we have become negligent in any of the above, and have not been exerting ourselves, we need to correct our course. God does not want us to be indifferent or halfhearted. It would be foolishness on our part if we kept postponing the work he has given us to do, thinking, I will get to it tomorrow as tomorrow never comes. We must awaken ourselves to the Great Commission that Jesus has given us.

Acts 20:35 English Standard Version (ESV)

³⁵ In all things I have shown you that by working hard in this way we must help the weak and remember the words of

the Lord Jesus, how he himself said, 'It is more blessed to give than to receive.'"

If we find joy in the fact we have offered a used coat to a homeless person, or a meal to a hungry family at a shelter; imagine what our joy will be if we play a role in getting another person on the path to eternal life. Imagine how our inner person will shine as we see this unbeliever become a believer. Imagine each time they learn something new, or finally grasp something that they have been struggling with, we will have a continued joy as they grow in the truth, and make it their own.

APPENDIX D Using the Bible When We Evangelize

Edward D. Andrews

The Word of God employs incredible power upon those who hear it, but only if they had a receptive heart or the evangelist was able to adjust that one's thinking. Once a person accepts the Bible as being the Word of God, it will carry more of an impact than anything that man has ever written. Therefore, it is highly important that we become proficient in the use of our Bible when witnessing to others. God's Word will enable us to sift through those not really wanting to know the truth, helping us to develop or discover right-hearted ones, enabling them to get on the path of salvation.

2 Timothy 3:16-17 New American Standard Bible (NASB)

[16] All Scripture is inspired by God and profitable for teaching, for reproof, for correction, for training in righteousness; [17] so that the man of God may be adequate, equipped for every good work.

Are we using the Bible while we do our personal study? Are we looking up the Scripture every time one is cited? Are we using the Bible when we are preparing for our congregation meetings? Are we then using the Bible once at the congregation meetings? Are we using the Bible when we try to witness informally to others? While this may not apply to you the reader, but one survey after another, shows that ninety percent of Christians are biblically illiterate. This means **(1)** they cannot use the book that they claim to be the Word of God. This means **(2)** that they are unable to look up Scriptures when talking with unbelievers. This means **(3)** they cannot defend the Bible as truly being the Word of God. This means **(4)** they are unable to explain the foundation beliefs of Scripture correctly. This means **(5)** they are unable to reason from the Scriptures, explaining and proving what is necessary for the listener to accept a belief as true. This means **(6)** that they have not been trained by their church to effectively communicate the Word of God.

If we are going to accomplish the things above, it means preparation on our part. Are we buying out the time to develop the skills needed to accomplish all six of the above points? If we are reading this book; then, our heart is seeking to do just that. We might be thinking that the above seems quite difficult to ascertain, but it is not as difficult as one might expect. If we will do the following for the next year of our Christian walk, we will be on our way to achieving all six of the above.

(1) Have a personal Bible study time of at least thirty minutes a day, preferably one hour.[48]

(2) Prepare for all Christian meetings.

(3) Look up Scriptures when they are not cited within the literature.

(4) Participate at the congregation meetings if that particular meeting allows it (e.g., Bible study class).

---

[48] In this study, you will be working through the Holman Old and New Testament Commentary volumes, as well as Bible Difficulties in the Book of Genesis: Answering the Bible Critics. These Bible Difficulty volumes will enable you to have answers to defend the Bible as the Word of God.

(5) Use the Bible whenever opportunity presents itself. Do not paraphrase a Scripture, pull out the Bible, look it up, and hold it in front of the person, read it aloud.

(6) Every time we learn something new, share it with at least one person, and not on the internet. Explain it as though it were a teaching moment. Try to do this with as many Christian friends as possible, making it a different person each time.

(7) At least once a week, find a relatively or completely new person at the meeting, and pull them aside to share something biblically exciting.[49] See the example below about Samson.

(8) Continue to read this series, *The Christian Evangelist*, as it will help us to develop our skills in effective communication.

(9) Look for opportunities to witness to unbelievers after a few months of doing the above. If possible, find a friend, who will be doing the above as well. The best-case scenario is that the congregation might choose to start an evangelism program.

Something New to Share

Judges 16:2-3 English Standard Version (ESV)

² The **Gazites** were told, "Samson has come here." And they surrounded the place and set an ambush for him all

---

[49] This will give you the experience of talking to strangers about the Bible, and develop your skills as a teacher, because you have to hone them to be effective on one with little Bible knowledge.

night at **the gate of the city**. They kept quiet all night, saying, "Let us wait till the light of the morning; then we will kill him." ³ But Samson lay till midnight, and at midnight he arose and **took hold of the doors of the gate of the city and the two posts, and pulled them up**, bar and all, and **put them on his shoulders** and **carried them to the top of the hill that is in front of Hebron**.

Image 2 City gate from Balawat—Zondervan Illustrated Bible Backgrounds

Every Christian is aware of Samson's superhuman strength that he received through God. However, some biblical accounts come to life when the reader is aware of the background information. What Samson pulled out of the ground and threw on his shoulders at Judges 16:2-3, weighted minimum of 400-500 pounds, with some suggesting closer to 2,000 pounds. If this feat of strength is not enough to grow our appreciation of Samson' great power, the simple statement that he "carried them to the top of the hill that is in front of Hebron," will do just that. Gaza, the city mentioned here is at sea level, while Hebron is about 3,000 feet above sea level, a serious climb indeed! However, there is more. Hebron is 37 miles from Gaza, uphill all the way! Knowing the weight of the gate and posts, the distance traveled, and that it was uphill, makes Samson's colossal feat take on a completely new magnitude, does it not?

If the reader will carry out the above for one year, which is really nothing more than four things every Christian should be doing anyway: (1) have a personal Bible study, (2) prepare for Christian meetings, (3) share the things we are learning, and (4) use our Bible. If we do not put knowledge in our head, there will be nothing to draw on when it comes time to share biblical truths.

There is no joy or excitement when we are unprepared, no matter what it is. Take a moment to remember the first day on any job. It was so frightening, and we were tense all day. Now, remember one year into that job. After just one year, we were completely competent and experienced to the point, we did most things subconsciously, not even giving much thought to it. Now, after one year of the above-suggested nine practices, imagine that we are sitting at a food court reading our Bible in the shopping mall, when a person at the next table says, 'I don't believe in the Bible.' Your heart does not even miss a beat, you simply respond, 'Why, have you always felt that way?' He responds with several reasons,

(1) 'the Bible contradicts itself,'

(2) 'It is full of errors,'

(3) 'it is a book by men nothing more,'

(4) 'everyone has his own interpretation of the Bible,'

(5) 'it is not practical for our day,'

(6) 'and while I agree that the Bible offers good advice on some things, I do not believe there is such thing as absolute truth.'

Even his extensive list of criticisms of the Bible does not intimidate us at this point. From his perspective, all of these seem true. He does not seem to be one looking to argue, but rather one who wishes his list were not true. We take a deep breath and ask, 'can I address at least one of these concerns?' He says, 'sure, I would like to have answers to all of the errors and contradictions.' We pick up our lunch, move over to his table, and offer to address a few.

Over the next hour, we find that we can flip through the Bible, sharing one Scripture after another, referring to several archaeological points, giving some in-depth Bible backgrounds, and even referring to a few original language words. Moreover, we gave him the gist of how these so-called errors and contradictions are really Bible difficulties. In the end, we resolved four major Bible difficulties for him. He was so moved by our ability to effectively reason from the Scriptures; he is the one that asked, 'can I talk with you again?' The conversation ended with an exchange of contact information.

Psalm 119:162 English Standard Version (ESV)

[162] I rejoice at your word
like one who finds great spoil.

APPENDIX E Bible Difficulties Explained

Edward D. Andrews

IT SEEMS THAT the charge that the Bible contradicts itself has been made more and more in the last 20 years. Generally, those making such claims are merely repeating what they have heard, because most have not even read the Bible, let alone done an in-depth study of it. I do not wish, however, to set aside all concerns as though they have no merit. There are many who raise legitimate questions that seem, on the surface anyway, to be about well-founded contradiction. Sadly, these issues have caused many to lose their faith in God's Word, the Bible. The purpose of this series of books is, to help its readers to be able to defend the Bible against Bible critics (1 Pet 3:15), to contend for the faith (Jude 1:3), and help those, who have begun to doubt. Jude 1:22-23

Inerrancy: Can the Bible Be trusted?

If the Bible is the Word of God, it should be in complete agreement throughout; there should be no contradictions. Yet, the rational mind must ask, why is it that some passages appear to be contradictions when compared with others? For example, Numbers 25:9 tells us that 24,000 died from the scourge, whereas at 1 Corinthians 10:8, the apostle Paul says it was 23,000. This would seem to be a clear error. Before addressing such matters, let us first look at some background information.

Full inerrancy* in this book means that the original writings are fully without error in all that they state, as are the words. The words were not dictated (automaton), but the intended meaning is inspired, as are the words that convey that meaning. The Author allowed the writer to use his style of writing, yet controlled the meaning to the extent of not allowing the writer to choose a wrong word, which would not convey the intended meaning. Other more liberal-minded persons hold with *partial inerrancy*, which claims that as far as faith is concerned, this portion of God's Word is without error, but that there are historical, geographical, and scientific errors.

*There are several different levels of inerrancy. *Absolute Inerrancy* is the belief that the Bible is fully true and exact in every way; including not only relationships and doctrine, but also science and history. In other words, all information is completely exact. *Full Inerrancy* is the belief that the Bible was not written as a science or historical textbook, but is phenomenological, in that it is written from the human perspective. In other words, speaking of such things as the sun rising, the four corners of the earth, or the rounding off of number approximations are all from a human perspective. *Limited Inerrancy* is the belief that the Bible is meant only as a reflection of God's purposes and will, so the science and history is the understanding of the author's day, and is limited. Thus, the Bible is susceptible to errors in these areas. *Inerrancy of Purpose* is the belief that it is only inerrant in the purpose of bringing its readers to a saving faith. The Bible is not about facts, but about persons and relationships, thus, it is subject to error. *Inspired: Not Inerrant* is the belief that its authors are human and thus subject to human error. It should be noted that this author holds the position of full inerrancy.

For many today, the Bible is nothing more than a book written by men that are full of myths and legends, contradictions, and geographical, historical, and scientific errors. University professor Gerald A. Larue had this to say,

"The views of the writers as expressed in the Bible reflect the ideas, beliefs, and concepts current in their own times and are limited by the extent of knowledge in those times."[50] On the other hand, the Bible's claims are quite different.

> **2 Timothy 3:16, 17 (HCSB):** *All Scripture is inspired by God* and is profitable for teaching, for rebuking, for correcting, for training in righteousness, so that the man of God may be complete, equipped for every good work.

> **2 Peter 1:21 (ESV):** For no prophecy was ever produced by the will of man, but men spoke from God as they were carried along by the Holy Spirit.

The question remains as to whether the Bible is a book written by imperfect men and full of errors, or is written by imperfect men, but inspired of God. If the Bible is just another book by imperfect man, there is no hope for humankind. If it is inspired of God and without error, although penned by imperfect men, we have the hope of everything that it offers: a rich happy life now by applying counsel that lies within and the real life that is to come, everlasting life. This author contends that the Bible is inspired of God and free of human error, although written by imperfect humans.

Before we take on the critics who seem to sift the Scriptures looking for problematic verses, let us take a moment to reflect on how we should approach these alleged problem texts. The critic's argument goes something like this:

---

[50] Gerald Larue, "The Bible as a Political Weapon," *Free Inquiry* (Summer 1983): 39.

'If God does not err and the Bible is the Word of God, then the Bible should not have one single error or contradiction, yet it is full of errors and contradictions.' If the Bible is riddled with nothing but contradictions and errors as the critics would have us believe, why, out of 31,173 verses in the Bible, should there be only 2-3 thousand Bible difficulties that are called into question, this being less than ten percent of the whole?

First, let it be said that it is every Christian's obligation to get a deeper understanding of God's Word, just as the apostle Paul told Timothy:

1 Timothy 4:15, 16 (ESV): Practice these things, immerse yourself in them, so that all may see your progress. Keep a close watch on yourself and *on the teaching*. Persist in this, for by so doing you will save both yourself and your hearers.

Paul also told the Corinthians:

2 Corinthians 10:4, 5 (NET): For the weapons of our warfare are not human weapons, but are made powerful by God for tearing down strongholds. *We tear down arguments* and every arrogant obstacle that is raised up against the knowledge of God, and we *take every thought captive* to make it obey Christ.

Paul also told the Philippians:

Philippians 1:7 (ESV): It is right for me to feel this way about you all, because I hold you in my heart, for you are all partakers with me of grace, both in my imprisonment and *in the defense and confirmation of the gospel*.

In being able to defend against the modern-day critic, one has to be able to reason from the Scriptures and overturn the critic's argument(s) with mildness. If someone were to approach us about an alleged error or contradiction, what should we do? We should be frank and honest. If we do not have an answer, we should admit such. If the text in question gives the appearance of difficulty, we should admit this as well. If we are unsure as to how we should answer, we can simply say that we will look into it and get back with them, returning with a reasonable answer.

However, do not express disbelief and doubt to your critics, because they will be emboldened in their disbelief. It will put them on the offense and you on the defense. With great confidence, you can express that there is an answer. The Bible has withstood the test of 2,000 years of persecution and is the most printed book of all time, currently being translated into 2,287 languages. If these critical questions were so threatening, the Bible would not be the book that it is.

When you are pursuing the text in question, be unwavering in purpose, or resolved to find an answer. In some cases, it may take hours of digging to find the solution. Consider this: as you resolve these difficulties, you are also building your faith that God's Word is inerrant. Moreover, you will want to do preventative maintenance in your personal study. As you are doing your Bible reading, take note of these surface discrepancies and resolve them as you work your way through the Bible. Make this a part of your prayers as well. I recommend the following program. At the end of this chapter I list several books that deal with difficult passages. As you read your Bible from Genesis to Revelation, do not attempt it in one year; make it a four-year program. Use a good exegetical commentary like *The New International Commentary of the Old and New Testament*

(NICOT/NICNT) or *The New American Commentary* set, and *The Big Book of Bible Difficulties* by Norman L. Geisler, as well as *The Encyclopedia of Bible Difficulties* by Gleason Archer.

You should be aware that the originally written books were penned by men under inspiration. In fact, we do not have those originals, what textual scholars call autographs, but we do have thousands of copies. The copyists, however, were not inspired; therefore, as one might expect, throughout the first 1,400 years of copying, thousands of errors were transmitted into the texts that were being copied by imperfect hands that were not under inspiration when copying. Yet, the next 450 years saw a restoration of the text by textual scholars from around the world. Therefore, while many of our best literal translations today may not be inspired, they are a mirror-like reflection of the autographs by way of textual criticism.[51] Therefore, the fallacy could be with the copyist error that has simply not been weeded out. In addition, you must keep in mind that God's Word is without error, but our interpretation and understanding of that Word is not.

In this chapter, we are not going to take the space that we will in later chapters that are dedicated to one difficulty. Here, in short, we will address a number of them. Before looking at a few examples, it should be noted that the Bible is made up of 66 smaller books that were hand-written over a period of 1,600 years, having some 40 writers of various

---

[51] Textual criticism is the study of copies of any written work of which the autograph (original) is unknown, with the purpose of ascertaining the original text. Harold J. Green, Introduction to New Testament Textual Criticism (Peabody, MA: Hendrickson, 1995), 1.

trades such as shepherd, king, priest, tax collector, governor, physician, copyist, fisherman, and tentmaker. Therefore, it should not surprise us that some difficulties are encountered as we casually read through the Bible. Yet, if one were to take a deeper look, one would find that these difficulties are easily explained. Let us take a few pages to examine some passages that have been under attack.

Again, our objective here is not to be exhaustive, not even close. What we are looking to do is cover a few alleged contradictions and a couple of alleged mistakes. This is to give you, the reader, a small sampling of the reasonable answers that you will find in the recommended books at the end of the chapter. Remember, your Bible is a sword that you must use both offensively and defensively. One must wonder how long a warrior of ancient times would last who was not expertly trained in the use of his weapon. Let us look at a few scriptures that support our need to learn our Bible well so will be able to defend what we believe to be true.

When "false apostles, deceitful workmen, disguising themselves as apostles of Christ" were causing trouble in the congregation in Corinth, the apostle Paul wrote that under such circumstances, we are to *tear down their arguments* and *take every thought captive.* (2 Corinthians 10:4, 5; 11:13–15) All who present critical arguments against God's Word, or contrary to it, can have their arguments overturned by the Christian who is able and ready to defend that Word in mildness.—2 Timothy 2:24–26.

1 Peter 3:15: But in your hearts honor Christ the Lord as holy, *always being prepared* to make a *defense to anyone* who asks you for a reason for the hope that is in you; yet do it with *gentleness and respect.*

Peter says that we need to be prepared to make a *defense*. The Greek word behind the English 'defense' is *apologia*, which is actually a legal term that refers to the defense of a defendant in court. Our English apologetics is just what Peter spoke of, having the ability to give a reason to any who may challenge us, or to answer those who are not challenging us but who have honest questions that deserve to be answered.

2 Timothy 2:24, 25: And the Lord's servant must not be quarrelsome but kind to everyone, *able to teach*, patiently enduring evil, *correcting his opponents with gentleness*. God may perhaps grant them repentance leading to a knowledge [*epignosis*] of the truth.

Take a look at the Greek word (*epignosis*) behind the English "knowledge" in the above. "It is more intensive than *gnosis* (1108), knowledge, because it expresses a more thorough participation in the acquiring of knowledge on the part of the learner."[52] The requirement of all of the Lord's servants is that they be able to teach, but not in a quarrelsome way, and in a way to correct his opponents with mildness. Why? Because the purpose of it all is that by God, and through the Christian teacher, one may come to repentance and begin taking in an accurate knowledge of the truth.

---

[52] Spiros Zodhiates, *The Complete Word Study Dictionary: New Testament*, Electronic ed. (Chattanooga, TN: AMG Publishers, 2000, c1992, c1993), S. G1922.

Inerrancy: Practical Principles to Overcoming Bible Difficulties

Different Points of View

At times, you may have two different writers who are writing from two different points of view.

Numbers 35:14 (NIV): Give three on this side of the Jordan and three in Canaan as cities of refuge.

Joshua 22:4 (NIV): Now that the LORD your God has given your brothers rest as he promised, return to your homes in the land that Moses the servant of the LORD gave you on the other side of the Jordan.

Here we see that Moses is speaking about the east side of the Jordan when he says "on this side of the Jordan." Joshua, on the other hand, is also speaking about the east side of the Jordan when he says "on the other side of the Jordan." So, who is correct? Both are. When Moses was penning Numbers the Israelites had not yet crossed the Jordan River, so the east side was "this side," the side he was on. On the other hand, when Joshua penned his book, the Israelites had crossed the Jordan, so the east side was just as he had said, "on the other side of the Jordan."

A Careful Reading

At times, it may simply be a case of needing to slow down and carefully read the account, considering exactly what is being said.

Joshua 18:28 (NASB): And Zelah, Haeleph and the *Jebusite* (that is, *Jerusalem*), Gibeah, Kiriath; fourteen cities with their villages. This is the *inheritance of the sons of Benjamin* according to their families.

Judges 1:21 (NIV): The Benjamites, however, *failed to dislodge the Jebusites*, who were living in Jerusalem; to this day the Jebusites live there with the Benjamites.

Joshua 15:63 (NASB): Now as for the *Jebusites*, the inhabitants of *Jerusalem*, the sons of Judah *could not drive them out*; so the Jebusites live with the sons of Judah at Jerusalem until this day.

Judges 1:8, 9 (NASB): Then *the sons of Judah fought against Jerusalem and captured it* and struck it with the edge of the sword and set the city on fire. Afterward the sons of Judah went down to fight against the Canaanites living in the hill country and in the Negev and in the lowland.

2 Samuel 5:5–9 (NASB): At Hebron he *[David] reigned over Judah* seven years and six months, and in Jerusalem he reigned thirty-three years over all Israel and Judah. Now *the king and his men went to Jerusalem against the Jebusites*, the inhabitants of the land, and they said to David, "You shall not come in here, but the blind and lame will turn you away"; thinking, "David cannot enter here." Nevertheless, *David captured the stronghold of Zion*, that is the city of David. David said on that day, "Whoever would strike the Jebusites, let him reach the lame and the blind, who are hated by David's soul, through the water tunnel." Therefore, they say, "The blind or the lame shall not come into the house." Therefore, David lived in the stronghold and called it the city of David And David built all around from the Millo and inward.

There is no doubt that even the advanced Bible reader of many years can come away confused because the above accounts seem to be contradictory. In Joshua 18:28 and Judges 1:21, we see that Jerusalem was an inheritance of the tribe of Benjamin, yet the Benjamites were unable to conquer Jerusalem. But in Joshua 15:63 we see that the tribe of Judah could not conquer them either, with the reading giving the impression that it was a part of their inheritance. In Judges 1:8, however, Judah was eventually able to conquer Jerusalem and burn it with fire. Yet, to add even more to the confusion, we find at 2 Samuel 5:5–8 that David is said to have conquered Jerusalem hundreds of years later.

Now that we have the particulars, let us look at it more clearly. The boundary between Benjamin's inheritances ran right through the middle of Jerusalem. Joshua 8:28 is correct, in that what would later be called the "city of David" was in the territory of Benjamin, but it also in part crossed over the line into the territory of Judah, causing both tribes to go to war against this Jebusite city. It is also true that the tribe of Benjamin was unable to conquer the city and that the tribe of Judah eventually did. However, if you look at Judges 1:9 again, you will see that Judah did not finish the job entirely and moved on to conquer other areas. This allowed the remaining ones to regroup and form a resistance that neither Benjamin nor Judah could overcome, so these Jebusites remained until the time of David, hundreds of years later.

Intended Meaning of Writer

First, the Bible student needs to understand the level that the Bible intends to be exact in what is written. If Jim told a friend that 650 graduated with him from high school in 1984, it is not challenged, because it is all too clear that he is using rounded numbers and is not meaning to be exactly precise. This is how God's Word operates as well. Sometimes it means to be exact, at other times, it is simply rounding numbers, in other cases, the intention of the writer is a general reference, to give readers of that time and succeeding generations some perspective. Did Samuel, the author of judges, intend to pen a book on the chronology of Judges, or was his focus on the falling away, oppression, and the rescue by a judge, repeatedly. Now, it would seem that Jeremiah, the author of 1 Kings was more interested in giving his readers an exact number of years.

Acts 2:41 (ESV): So those who received his word were baptized, and there were added that day *about three thousand souls*.

As you can see here, numbers within the Bible are often used with approximations. This is a frequent practice even today, in both written works and verbal conversation.

Acts 7:2-3 (ESV): Brothers and fathers, hear me. The God of glory appeared to our father Abraham when he was in Mesopotamia, before he lived in Haran, and said to him, "Go out from your land and from your kindred and go into the land that I will show you."

If you were to check the Hebrew Scriptures at Genesis 12:1, you would find that what is claimed to have been said by God to Abraham is not quoted word-for-word; it is simply a paraphrase. This is a normal practice within Scripture and in writing in general.

Numbers 34:15 (ESV): The two tribes and the half-tribe have received their inheritance beyond the Jordan east of Jericho, toward the sunrise.

Just as you would read in today's local newspaper, the Bible writer has written from the human standpoint, how it appeared to him. The Bible also speaks of "to the end of the earth" (Psalm 46:9), "from the four corners of the earth" (Isa

11:12), and "the four winds of the earth" (Revelation 7:1). These are phrases that are still used today.

Unexplained Does Not Equal Unexplainable

Considering that there are 31,173 verses in the Bible, encompassing 66 books written by about 40 writers, ranging from shepherds, to kings, an army general, fishermen, tax collector, a physician and on and on, and being penned over a 1,600 year period, one does find a few hundred Bible difficulties (about one percent). However, 99 percent of those are explainable. Yet no one wants to be so arrogant to say that he can explain them all. It has nothing to do with the inadequacy of God's Word, but is based on human understanding. In many cases, science or archaeology and the field of custom and culture of ancient peoples has helped explain difficulties in hundreds of passages. Therefore, there may be less than one percent left to be answered, yet our knowledge of God's Word continues to grow.

Guilty Until Proven Innocent

This is exactly the perception that the critic has of God's Word. The legal principle of being "innocent until proven guilty" afforded mankind in courts of justice is withheld from the very Word of God. What is ironic here is that this policy has contributed to these Bible critics looking foolish over and over again when something comes to light that vindicates the portion of Scripture they are challenging.

Daniel 5:1 English Standard Version (ESV)

¹ King Belshazzar made a great feast for a thousand of his lords and drank wine in front of the thousand.

Bible critics had long claimed that Belshazzar was not known outside of the book Daniel; therefore, they argue that

Daniel was mistaken. Yet it hardly seems prudent to argue error from absence of outside evidence. Just because archaeology had not discovered such a person did not mean that Daniel was wrong, or that such a person did not exist. In 1854, some small clay cylinders were discovered in modern-day southern Iraq, which would have been the city of Ur in ancient Babylonia. The cuneiform documents were a prayer of King Nabonidus for "Bel-sar-ussur, my eldest son." These tablets also showed that this "Bel-sar-ussur" had secretaries as well as a household staff. Other tablets were discovered a short time later that showed that the kingship was entrusted to this eldest son as a coregent while his father was away.

> He entrusted the 'Camp' to his oldest (son), the firstborn [Belshazzar], the troops everywhere in the country he ordered under his (command). He let (everything) go, entrusted the kingship to him and, himself, he [Nabonidus] started out for a long journey, the (military) forces of Akkad marching with him; he turned towards Tema (deep) in the west."[53]

Ignoring Literary Styles

The Bible is a diverse book when it comes to literary styles: narrative, poetic, prophetic, and apocalyptic; also containing parables, metaphors, similes, hyperbole, and other figures of speech. Too often, these alleged errors are the result of a reader taking a figure of speech as literal, or reading a parable as though it is a narrative.

Matthew 24:35: Heaven and earth will pass away, but my words will not pass away.

---

[53] J. Pritchard, ed., *Ancient Near Eastern Texts* (1974), 313.

If some do not recognize that they are dealing with a figure of speech, they are bound to come away with the wrong meaning. Some have concluded from Matthew 24:35 that Jesus was speaking of an eventual destruction of the earth. This is hardly the case, as his listeners would not have understood it that way based on their understanding of the Old Testament. They would have understood that he was simply being emphatic about the words he spoke, using hyperbole. What he was conveying is that his words are more enduring than heaven and earth, and with heaven and earth being understood as eternal, this merely conveyed even more so that Jesus' words could be trusted.

Two Accounts of the Same Incident

If you were to speak to officers that take accident reports for their police department, you would find that there is cohesion in the accounts, but each person has merely witnessed aspects that have stood out to them. We will see that this is the case as well with the examples below:

Matthew 8:5: When he entered Capernaum, *a centurion came forward to him*, appealing to him.

Luke 7:3: When *the centurion* heard about Jesus, he *sent to him elders of the Jews*, asking him to come and heal his servant.

Immediately we see the problem of whether the centurion or the elders of the Jews spoke with Jesus. The solution is not really hidden from us. Which of the two accounts is the more detailed account? You are correct if you said Luke. The centurion sent the elders of the Jews to represent him to Jesus, so; that whatever response Jesus might give, it would be as though he were addressing the centurion; therefore, Matthew gave his readers the basic thought, not seeing the need of mentioning the elders of the Jews aspect. This is how a representative was viewed in the first century, just as some countries see ambassadors today as being the very person they represent. So both Matthew and Luke are correct.

Man's Fallible Interpretations

Inspiration by God is infallible, without error. Imperfect man and his interpretations over the centuries, as bad as many of them have been, should not cast a shadow over God's inspired Word. The entire Word of God has one meaning and one meaning only for every penned word, which is what God willed to be conveyed by the human writer he chose to use.

The Autograph Alone Is Inspired and Inerrant

It has been argued by conservative scholars that only the autograph manuscripts were inspired and inerrant, not the copying of those manuscripts over the next 3,000 years for the Old Testament and 1,500 years for the New Testament. While I would agree with this position as well, it should be noted that we do not possess the autographs, so to argue that they are inerrant is to speak of nonexistent documents. However, it should be further understood that through the science of textual criticism, we can establish a mirror reflection of the autograph manuscripts. B. F. Westcott, F. J. A. Hort, F. F. Bruce, and many other textual scholars would agree with Norman L Geisler's assessment: "The New Testament, then, has not only survived in more manuscripts than any other book from antiquity, but it has survived in a purer form than any other great book—*a form that is 99.5 percent pure.*"[54]

An example of a copyist error can be found in Luke's genealogy of Jesus at Luke 3:35–37. In verse 37 you will find a Cainan, and in verse 36 you will find a second Cainan between Arphaxad (Arpachshad) and Shelah. As one can see from most footnotes in different study Bibles, the Cainan in verse 36 is seen as a scribal error, and is not found in the Hebrew Old Testament, the Samaritan Pentateuch, or the Aramaic Targums, but is found in the Greek Septuagint. (Genesis 10:24; 11:12, 13; 1 Chronicles 1:18, but not 1 Chronicles 1:24) It seems quite unlikely that it was in the earlier copies of the Septuagint, because the first-century Jewish historian Josephus lists Shelah next as the son of Arphaxad, and Josephus normally followed the Septuagint.[55] So one might ask why this second Cainan is found in the translations at all if this is the case? The manuscripts that do contain this second Cainan are some of the best manuscripts that are used in establishing the original text: 01 B L A[1] 33 (Kainam); A 038 044 0102 A[13] (Kainan).

Look at the Context

Many alleged inconsistencies disappear by simply looking at the context. Taking words out of context can distort their meaning. *Merriam-Webster's Collegiate Dictionary* defines context as "the parts of a discourse that surround a word or

---

[54] Norman L. Geisler and William E. Nix: *A General Introduction to the Bible* (Chicago, Moody Press, 1980), 367. (Emphasis is mine.)

[55] *Jewish Antiquities*, I, 146 [vi, 4].

passage and can throw light on its meaning."[56] Context can also be "the circumstances or events that form the environment within which something exists or takes place." If we were to look in a thesaurus for a synonym, we would find "background" for this second meaning. At 2 Timothy 2:15, the apostle Paul brings home the point of why context is so important: "Do your best to present yourself to God as one approved, a worker who has no need to be ashamed, rightly handling the word of truth."

Ephesians 2:8, 9: For by grace you have been saved through faith. And this is not your own doing; it is the gift of God, not a result of works, so that no one may boast.

James 2:26: For as the body apart from the spirit is dead, so also faith apart from works is dead.

So, which is it? Is salvation possible by faith and not works as Paul wrote to the Ephesians, or is faith dead without works as James wrote to his readers? As our subtitle brings out, let us look at the context. In the letter to the Ephesians the apostle Paul is speaking to the Jewish Christians who were looking to the works of the Mosaic Law as a means to salvation, a righteous standing before God. Paul was telling these legalistic Jewish Christians that this is not so. In fact, this would invalidate Christ's ransom, because there would have been no need for it if one could achieve salvation by meticulously keeping the Mosaic Law. (Romans 5:18) But James was writing to those in a congregation who were concerned with their status before other men, who were looking for prominent positions within the congregation, and

---

[56] Merriam-Webster, Inc: *Merriam-Webster's Collegiate Dictionary*. Eleventh ed. (Springfield, Mass.: Merriam-Webster, Inc. 2003).

not taking care of those that were in need. (James 2:14–17) So, James is merely addressing those who call themselves Christian, but in name only. No person could truly be a Christian and not possess some good works, such as feeding the poor, helping the elderly. This type of work was an evident demonstration of one's Christian personality. Paul was in perfect harmony with James on this.—Romans 10:10; 1 Corinthians 15:58; Ephesians 5:15, 21–33; 6:15; 1 Timothy 4:16; 2 Timothy 4:5; Hebrews 10:23–25.

Inerrancy: Are There Contradictions?

Below I will follow this pattern. I will list the critic's argument first, followed by the text of difficulty, and conclude with an answer to the critic. What should be kept at the forefront of our mind is this: one is simply looking for the best answer, not absoluteness. If there is a reasonable answer to a Bible difficulty, why are the critics able to set them aside with ease? Because they start with the premise that this is not the Word of God, but only a book by imperfect men and full of contradictions; thus, the bias toward errors has blinded their judgment.

Critic: The critic would argue that there was an Adam and Eve, and an Abel who was now dead, so, where did Cain get his wife?

Genesis 4:17 (NET): Cain had marital relations with his wife, and she became pregnant and gave birth to Enoch. Cain was building a city, and he named the city after his son Enoch.

Answer: If one were to read a little further along they would come to the realization that Adam had a son named Seth; it further adds that Adam "became father to sons *and* *daughters.*" (Genesis 5:4) Adam lived for a total of 800 years after fathering Seth, giving him ample opportunity to father many more sons and daughters. So it could be that Cain married one of his sisters. If he waited until one of his brothers and sisters had a daughter, he could have married one of his nieces once she was old enough. In the beginning, humans were closer to perfection; this explains why they lived longer and why at that time there was little health risk of genetic defects in the case of children born to closely related parents, in contrast to how it is today. As time passed, genetic defects increased and life spans decreased. Adam lived to see 930 years. Yet Shem, who lived after the Flood, died at 600 years, while Shem's son Arpachshad only lived 438 years, dying before his father died. Abraham saw an even greater decrease in that he only lived 175 years, while his grandson Jacob was 147 years when he died. Thus, due to increasing imperfection, God prohibited the marriage of closely related people under the Mosaic Law because of the likelihood of genetic defects.—Leviticus 18:9.

Critic: If God is here hardening Pharaoh's heart, what exactly makes Pharaoh responsible for the decisions he makes?

Exodus 4:21 (RSV): And the LORD said to Moses, "When you go back to Egypt, see that you do before Pharaoh all the miracles that I have put in your power. But I will harden his heart, so that he will not let the people go."

Answer: This is actually a prophecy. God knew that what he was about to do would contribute to a stubborn and obstinate Pharaoh, who was going to be unwilling to change or give up the Israelites so they could go off to worship their God. So this is not stating what God is going to do; it is prophesying that Pharaoh's heart will harden because of the actions of God. The fact is, Pharaoh allowed his own heart to harden because he was determined not to agree with Moses' wishes or accept Jehovah's request to let the people go. Moses tells us at Exodus 7:13 (ESV) that "Pharaoh's heart was hardened, and he would not listen to them, as the LORD had said." Again, at 8:15 we read: "When Pharaoh saw that there was a respite, he hardened his heart and would not listen to them, as the LORD had said."

Critic: The Israelites had just received the Ten Commandments, with one commandment being: "You shall not make for yourself a carved image, or any likeness of anything that is in heaven above, or that is in the earth beneath, or that is in the water under the earth." Therefore, how is the bronze serpent not a violation of this commandment?

Numbers 21:9: So Moses made a bronze serpent and set it on a pole. And if a serpent bit anyone, he would look at the bronze serpent and live.

Answer: First, an idol is "a representation or symbol of an object of worship; *broadly*: a false god."[57] Second, it should be noted that not all images are idols. The bronze serpent was not made for the purpose of worship, or for some passionate devotion or veneration. There were times, however, when images were created with absolutely no intention of it receiving devotion, veneration, or worship, yet were later made into objects of veneration. That is exactly what happened with the copper serpent that Moses had

---

[57] Merriam-Webster, Inc: *Merriam-Webster's Collegiate Dictionary*. Eleventh ed. (Springfield, Mass.: Merriam-Webster, Inc., 2003).

formed in the wilderness. Many centuries later, "in the third year of Hoshea son of Elah, king of Israel, Hezekiah the son of Ahaz, king of Judah, began to reign. He removed the high places and broke the pillars and cut down the Asherah. And he broke in pieces the bronze serpent that Moses had made; for until those days the people of Israel had made offerings to it (it was called Nehushtan)."—2 Kings 18:1, 4.

Critic: Deuteronomy 15:11 (NET) says: *"There will never cease to be some poor people in the land;* therefore, I am commanding you to make sure you open your hand to your fellow Israelites who are needy and poor in your land." Is this not a contradiction of Deuteronomy 15:4? Will there be no poor among the Israelites, or will there be poor among them? Which is it?

Deuteronomy 15:4 (NET): However, there should not be any poor among you, for the LORD will surely bless you in the land that he is giving you as an inheritance.

Answer: If you look at the context, Deuteronomy 15:4 is stating that if the Israelites obey Jehovah's command to take care of the poor, "there should not be any poor among" them. Thus, for every poor person, there will be one to take care of that need. If an Israelite fell on hard times, there was to be a fellow Israelite ready to step in to help him through those hard times. Verse 11 stresses the truth of the imperfect world since the rebellion of Adam and inherited sin: there will always be poor among mankind, the Israelites being no different. However, the difference with God's people is that those who were well off were to offset conditions for those who fell on difficult times. This is not to be confused with the socialistic welfare systems in the world today. Those Jews were hard-working men, who labored from sunup to sundown to take care of their families. But if disease overtook their herd or unseasonal weather brought about failed crops, an Israelite could sell himself into the service of a fellow Israelite for a period of time; thereafter, he would be back on his feet. And many years down the road, he may very well do the same for another Israelite who fell on difficult times.

Critic: Joshua 11:23 says that Joshua took the land according to what God had spoken to Moses and handed it on to the nation of Israel as planned. But in Joshua 13:1, God is telling Joshua that he has grown old and much of the Promised Land has yet to be taken possession of. How can both be true? Is this not a contradiction?

Joshua 11:23: So Joshua took the whole land, according to all that the LORD had spoken to Moses. And Joshua gave it for an inheritance to Israel according to their tribal allotments. And the land had rest from war.

Joshua 13:1: Now Joshua was old and advanced in years, and the LORD said to him, "You are old and advanced in years, and there remains yet very much land to possess."

Answer: No, it is not a contradiction. When the Israelites were to take the land, it was to take place in two different stages: 1) the nation as a whole was to go to war and defeat the 31 kings of this land; thereafter, each Israelite tribe was to take their part of the land based on their individual actions. (Joshua 17:14–18; 18:3) Joshua fulfilled his role, which is expressed in 11:23, while the individual tribes did not complete their campaigns, which is expressed in 13:1. Even though the individual tribes failed to live up to taking their portion, the remaining Canaanites posed no real threat. Joshua 21:44, *ASV*, reads: "Jehovah gave them rest round about."

Critic: The critic would point out that John 1:18 clearly says that *"no one has ever seen God,"* while Exodus 24:10 explicitly states that Moses and Aaron, Nadab and Abihu, and seventy of the elders of Israel *"saw the God of Israel."* Worse still, God informs them in Exodus 33:20: "You cannot see my face, for man shall not see me and live." The critic with his knowing smile says: 'This is a blatant contradiction.'

John 1:18 (NASB): No one has seen God at any time; the only begotten God who is in the bosom of the Father, He has explained *Him*. (Italics NASB.)

Exodus 24:10: And they saw the God of Israel. There was under his feet as it were a pavement of sapphire stone, like the very heaven for clearness.

Exodus 33:20: "But," he said, "you cannot see my face, for man shall not see me and live."

Answer: Exodus 33:20 is one-hundred percent correct: No human could see Jehovah God and live. The apostle Paul at Colossians 1:15 tells us that Christ is the image of the invisible God, and the writer informs us at Hebrews 1:3 that Jesus is the "exact representation of His nature." Yet if you were to read the account of Saul of Tarsus (the apostle Paul), you would see that a mere partial manifestation of Christ's glory blinded Saul (Acts 9:1–18).

When the Bible says that Moses and others have seen God, it is not speaking of *literally* seeing him, because first of all He is an invisible spirit person. It is a *manifestation* of his glory, which is an act of showing or demonstrating his presence, making himself perceptible to the human mind. In fact, it is generally an angelic representative that stands in his place and not him personally. Exodus 24:16 informs us that "the glory of the LORD dwelt on Mount Sinai," not the LORD himself personally. When texts such as Exodus 24:10 explicitly state that Moses and Aaron, Nadab and Abihu, and seventy of the elders of Israel "*saw the God of Israel*," it is this "glory of the LORD," an angelic representative. This is shown to be the case at Luke 2:9, which reads: "And *an angel of the Lord* appeared to them, and *the glory of the Lord shone around them* [the shepherds], and they were filled with fear."

Many Bible difficulties are cleared up elsewhere in Scripture; for example, in the New Testament you will find a text clarifying a difficulty from the Old Testament, such as Acts 7:53, which refers to those "who received the law *as delivered by angels* and did not keep it." Support comes from Paul at Galatians 3:19: "Why then the law? It was added because of transgressions, until the offspring should come to whom the promise had been made, and it was put in place through angels by an intermediary." The writer of Hebrews chimes in at 2:2 with "For since the message *declared by angels* proved to be reliable, and every transgression or disobedience received a just retribution. . . ." As we travel back to Exodus again, to 19:19 specifically, we find support that it was not God's own voice that Moses heard; no, it was an angelic representative, for it reads: "Moses was speaking and God was answering him with a voice." Exodus 33:22–23 also helps us to appreciate that it was the back of these angelic representatives of Jehovah that Moses saw: "While my glory passes by . . . Then I will take away my hand, and you shall see my back, but my face shall not be seen."

Exodus 3:4 states: "God called to him out of the bush, 'Moses, Moses!' And he said, 'Here I am.'" Verse 6 informs us: "I am the God of your father, the God of Abraham, the God of Isaac, and the God of Jacob." Yet, in verse 2 we read:

"And the angel of the LORD appeared to him in a flame of fire out of the midst of a bush." Here is another example of using God's Word to clear up what seems to be unclear or difficult to understand at first glance. Thus, while it speaks of the LORD making a direct appearance, it is really an angelic representative. Even today, we hear such comments as 'the president of the United States is to visit the Middle East later this week.' However, later in the article it is made clear that he is not going personally, but it is one of his high ranking representatives. Let us close with two examples, starting with Genesis 32:24–30:

> And Jacob was left alone. And a man wrestled with him until the breaking of the day. When the man saw that he did not prevail against Jacob, he touched his hip socket, and Jacob's hip was put out of joint as he wrestled with him. Then he said, "Let me go, for the day has broken." But Jacob said, "I will not let you go unless you bless me." And he said to him, "What is your name?" And he said, "Jacob." Then he said, "Your name shall no longer be called Jacob, but Israel, for you have striven with God and with men, and have prevailed." Then Jacob asked him, "Please tell me your name." But he said, "Why is it that you ask my name?" And there he blessed him. So Jacob called the name of the place Peniel, saying, "For I have seen God face to face, and yet my life has been delivered."

It is all too obvious here that this man is simply a materialized angel in the form of a man, another angelic representative of Jehovah God. Moreover, the reader of this book should have taken in that the Israelites as a whole saw these angelic representatives, and spoke of them as though they were dealing directly with Jehovah God himself.

This proved to be the case in the second example found in the book of Judges where an angelic representative visited Manoah and his wife. Like the above mentioned account, Manoah and his wife treated this angelic representative as if he were Jehovah God himself: "And Manoah said to the angel of the LORD, 'What is your name, so that, when your words come true, we may honor you?' And the angel of the LORD said to him, 'Why do you ask my name, seeing it is wonderful?' Then Manoah knew that he was the angel of the LORD. And Manoah said to his wife, "We shall surely die, *for we have seen God.*"—Judges 13:3–22.

Inerrancy: Are There Mistakes?

I have addressed the alleged contradictions, so it would seem that our job is done here, right? Not hardly. Yes, there are just as many who claim that the Bible is full of mistakes.

Critic: Matthew 27:5 states that Judas hanged himself, whereas Acts 1:18 says that "falling headlong he burst open in the middle and all his bowels gushed out."

Matthew 27:5: And throwing down the pieces of silver into the temple, he departed, and he went and hanged himself.

Acts 1:18: Now this man acquired a field with the reward of his wickedness, and falling headlong he burst open in the middle and all his bowels gushed out.

Answer: Neither Matthew, nor Luke made a mistake. What you have is Matthew giving the reader the manner in which Judas committed suicide. On the other hand, Luke is giving the reader of Acts, the result of that suicide. Therefore, instead of a mistake, we have two texts that complement each other, really giving the reader the full picture. Judas came to a tree alongside a cliff that had rocks below. He tied the rope to a branch and the other end around his neck, and jumped over the edge of the cliff in an attempt at hanging himself. One of two things could have happened: (1) the limb broke plunging him to the rocks below, or (2) the rope broke with the same result, and he burst open onto the rocks below.

Critic: The apostle Paul made a mistake when he quotes how many people died.

Numbers 25:9: Nevertheless, those who died by the plague were twenty-four thousand.

1 Corinthians 10:8: We must not indulge in sexual immorality as some of them did, and twenty-three thousand fell in a single day.

Answer: We must keep in mind the above principle that we spoke of, the *Intended Meaning of the Writer*. We live in a far more precise age today, where specificity is highly important. However, we round large numbers off (even estimate) all the time: "there were 237,000 people in Time Square last night." The simplest answer is that the number of people slain was in between 23,000 and 24,000, and both writers rounded the number off. However, there is even another possibility, because the book of Numbers specifically speaks of "all the chiefs of the people" (25:4-5), which could account for the extra 1,000, which is mentioned in Numbers 24,000. Thus, you have the people killing the chiefs of the people and the plague killing the people. Therefore, both books are correct.

Critic: After 215 years in Egypt, the descendants of Jacob arrived at the Promised Land. As you recall they sinned against God and were sentenced to forty years in the wilderness. But once they entered the Promised Land, they buried Joseph's bones "at Shechem, in the piece of land that *Jacob bought* from the sons of Hamor the father of Shechem," as stated at Joshua 24:32. Yet, when Stephen had to defend himself before the Jewish religious leaders, he said that Joseph was buried "in the tomb that *Abraham had bought* for a sum of silver from the sons of Hamor." Therefore, at once it appears that we have a mistake on the part of Stephen.

Acts 7:15, 16: And Jacob went down into Egypt, and he died, he and our fathers, and they were carried back to Shechem and laid *in the tomb* that *Abraham had bought* for a sum of silver *from the sons of Hamor in Shechem*.

Genesis 23:17, 18: So the field of *Ephron* in Machpelah, which was to the east of Mamre, the field with the cave that was in it and all the trees that were in the field, throughout its whole area, was made over *to Abraham* as a possession in the presence of the Hittites, before all who went in at the gate of his city.

Genesis 33:19: And from *the sons of Hamor*, Shechem's father, he [*Jacob*] *bought* for a hundred pieces of money *the piece of land* on which he had pitched his tent.

Joshua 24:32: As for the bones of Joseph, which the people of Israel brought up from Egypt, they *buried them at Shechem*, in the *piece of land* that *Jacob bought* from the *sons of Hamor the father of Shechem* for a hundred pieces of money. It became an inheritance of the descendants of Joseph.

Answer: If we look back to Genesis 12:6-7, we will find that Abraham's first stop after entering Canaan from Haran was Shechem. It is here that Jehovah told Abraham: "To your offspring I will give this land." At this point Abraham built an altar to Jehovah. It seems reasonable that Abraham would need to purchase this land that had not yet been given to his offspring. While it is true that the Old Testament does not mention this purchase, it is likely that Stephen would be aware of such by way of oral tradition. As Acts chapter seven demonstrates, Stephen had a wide-ranging knowledge of Old Testament history.

Later, Jacob would have had difficulty laying claim to the tract of land that his grandfather Abraham had purchased, because there would have been a new generation of inhabitants of Shechem. This would have been many years after Abraham moved further south and Isaac moved to Beersheba, and including Jacob's twenty years in Paddan-aram (Gen 28:6, 7). The simplest answer is that this land was not in use for about 120 years because of Abraham's extensive travels and Isaac's having moved away, leaving it unused; likely it was put to use by others. So, Jacob simply repurchased what Abraham had bought over a hundred years earlier. This is very similar to the time Isaac had to repurchase the well at Beersheba that Abraham had already purchased earlier. —Genesis 21:27–30; 26:26–32.

Genesis 33:18–20 tells us that 'Jacob bought this land for a hundred pieces of money, from the sons of Hamor.' This same transaction is also mentioned at Joshua 24:32, in reference to transporting Joseph's bones from Egypt, to be buried in Shechem.

We should also address the cave of Machpelah that Abraham had purchased in Hebron from Ephron the Hittite. The word "tomb" is not mentioned until Joshua 24:32, and is in reference to the tract of land in Shechem. Nowhere in the Old Testament does it say that Abraham bought a "tomb." The cave of Machpelah obtained by Abraham would eventually become a family tomb, receiving Sarah's body and, eventually, his own, and those of Isaac, Rebekah, Jacob, and Leah. (Genesis 23:14–19; 25:9; 49:30, 31; 50:13) Gleason L. Archer, Jr., concludes this Bible difficulty, saying:

> The reference to a *mnema* ("tomb") in connection with Shechem must either have been proleptic [to anticipate] for the later use of that shechemite tract for Joseph's tomb (i.e., 'the tomb that Abraham bought' was intended to imply 'the tomb location that Abraham bought"); or else conceivably the dative relative pronoun *ho* was intended elliptically [omission] for *en to topo ho onesato Abraam* ("in the place that Abraham bought") as describing the location of the *mnema* near the Oak of Moreh right outside Shechem. Normally Greek would have used the relative-locative adverb *hou* to express 'in which' or 'where'; but this would have left *onesato* ("bought") without an object in its own clause, and so *ho* was much more suitable in this context. (Archer 1982, 379–81)

Another solution could be that Jacob is being viewed as a representative of Abraham, for he is the grandson of Abraham. This was quite appropriate in Biblical times, to attribute the purchase to Abraham as the Patriarchal family head.

Critic: 2 Samuel 24:1 says that God moved David to count the Israelites, while 1 Chronicles 21:1 Satan, or a resister did. This would seem to be a clear mistake on the part of one of these authors.

2 Samuel 24:1: And again the anger of Jehovah was kindled against Israel, and he moved David against them, saying, Go, number Israel and Judah.

1 Chronicles 21:1: And Satan stood up against Israel, and moved David to number Israel.

Answer: In this period of David's reign, Jehovah was very displeased with Israel, and therefore he did not prevent Satan from bringing this sin on them. Often in Scripture, it is spoken of as though God did something when he allowed an event to take place. For example, it is said that God 'hardened Pharaoh's heart' (Exodus 4:21), when he actually allowed the Pharaoh's heart to harden.

Inerrancy: Are There Scientific Errors?

There are over a dozen different interpretations concerning the creative days of Genesis. Herein we will consider the main four in an effort to make our point. First, there is the *young earth view* that asserts that all physical creation was produced in just six literal 24-hour days sometime between 6,000 and 10,000 years ago. Second, there is the *day-age view* that asserts that each creative day is to be understood figuratively as creative periods of unknown durations of time. According to this view the earth is millions of years old, and the universe is billions of years old. Third, there is the *restoration view* (gap theory) that asserts that there is a large gap of time between Genesis 1:1 and 1:2. Fourth, there is the *literary framework view* that asserts that

God was not having Moses address how He created the world, nor the length of time in which to do such. This view holds that this account in Genesis 1 is merely a literary outline that summarizes a theology of creation. This so-called "seven day framework" is not to be understood in a literal sense of order and chronology, but is a literary device expressing God's involvement in creation and the Sabbath. Different Evangelical Christian scholars hold all four of these views; however, the author of this book dismisses three of these as being contrary to Scripture and science. We will discuss the first two views listed above in more detail below.[58]

I do not believe that those who hold to the young-earth view of creationism have the evidence to support their case, nor do they even speak in terms of evidence. Why? Most of the young-earth commentators attempt to disprove the day-age view by using many words like "possibly," "could be," "may be," and so on. In addition, I do not believe they look at the evidence without theological bias. Professor Kirk Wise writes:

> I am a young-age creationist because that is my understanding of the Scripture. As I shared with my professors years ago when I was in college, if all the evidence in the universe turns against creationism, I would be the first to admit it, but I would still be a creationist because that is what the Word of God seems to indicate. Here I must stand. (Ashton, 2001)[59]

---

[58] For a more in-depth understanding of these for creative views, see Gregory A. Boyd and Paul R. Eddy, *Across the Spectrum* (Grand Rapids, Baker Academic, 2002), 50–73.

[59] http://richarddawkins.net/articles/115.

It shows theological bias when he states that no evidence will change his mind. Just as in the case of Galileo, theologians cast doubt on the Bible by ignoring scientific evidence. The Bible was not out of harmony with the truth that the earth revolves around the sun and not the other way. God's Word needed no revision. It was the Roman Catholic Church's misinterpretation of the Bible that caused the problem. As one grows in understanding of physics, biology, and chemistry (as is also true with history, ancient languages, and manuscripts), one may need to revise conclusions derived from previous knowledge. When knowledge increases, it calls for humility to make adjustments in ones thinking.

To suggest, as do many conservative Christians, that one needs to read the Bible in a plain way (*sensus plenoir*) is quite misleading, as though one would never consider otherwise. Galileo's own words to a pupil said it well: "Even though Scripture cannot err, its interpreters and expositors can, in various ways. One of these, very serious and very frequent, would be when they always want to stop at the purely literal sense."[60] Professor Kirk Wise argues that because Genesis chapter one was written as historical narrative, it disallows an interpretation that has millions of years involved. This is hardly the case, for he goes on to admit that other historical narratives contain imbedded material that is not to be taken literally. Moreover, it is implied that one who accepts long creative periods must also believe the Big Bang theory, and believe that fossils are millions of years old, and believe in other facets of Evolution. This is simply untrue.

---

[60] Letter from Galileo to Benedetto Castelli, December 21, 1613.

Simply put, Genesis 1:1 says: "In the beginning God created the heavens and the earth." (ESV) This would include our home, the earth, and our solar system and galaxy that King David referred to when he looked into the night sky and wrote: "When I look at your heavens, the work of your fingers, the moon and the stars, which you have set in place, what is man that you are mindful of him, and the son of man that you care for him?" (Psalm 8:3, 4, *ESV*) It would also include all the billions of universes that David was unable to see with his naked eye. Therefore, all this came *before* the first day of creative preparation for life on the earth that starts in Genesis 1:3, as would also be the case with the description of the earth as found in verse 2. It is not until we get to Genesis 1:3–5 that Moses starts to expound on the first day of creation specifically in respect to the earth.

What does this mean? It means that regardless of how long you may feel the creative days were, verses 1 and 2 are covering things that existed prior to the start of the events described in the successive creative days. Therefore, it takes nothing away from the Bible when geologists state that the earth is four billion years old, or astronomers who have calculated the age of the universe say it is at least 14–20 billion years old. For the Christian to argue with science is only history repeating itself, as you will see before this chapter closes. Again, Genesis chapter one, verses 1 and 2, are outside the events of the creative days, which are simply a summary of the steps taken to transform the condition of verse 2 into the habitable earth in which the animals and Adam and Eve were created.

Now that we have settled the controversy between science and the *erroneous* interpretations of man's tradition that the universe and earth were created in only six literal days, we should clear the air over the age and origin of the sedimentary geological strata. Many have postulated that it was formed at the time of the flood of Noah. This answer is not to be found in God's Word. Those who hold to the young-earth view (6,000–10,000 years old), work very hard to try to reconcile the geologic column and the fossils of dinosaurs and such, in which they try to overcome evidence that shows the earth is millions of years old. What is now known and acknowledged by science is that the geological record does *not* contain a series of gradual and progressive stages of fossils from one species to another. Actually, the fossil record supports the creation account in that new species appear suddenly on the scene within this geological column, having absolutely no connection with any other species. The problem with young-earth proponents is that they are unable to use this information because it will not fit with their belief that all land and sea animals were created in two 24-hour days. This is not to say that this publication accepts the idea that the sea and land animals have existed for untold hundreds of millions of years, but it does not negate that the fifth and sixth creative days were possibly many thousands of years long, having flying and sea creatures, and land animals being created throughout, as well as dinosaurs.

What exactly does the Bible reveal? It says plainly that Jehovah God is the "fountain of life." (Psalm 36:9) In other words, life did not come from nothing, and then develop gradually in some evolutionary process over billions of years. Additionally, God's Word says that everything was created according to its kind. (Genesis 1:11, 21, 24) And finally, the Bible does provide the time period of man's creation, some 6,000 years ago. On this, both archaeology and Biblical chronology are not far off from each other. Creation is clearly stated within God's Word, and can be understood in relation to the correct study and interpretation of its texts, in light of factual science, astronomy, physics, chemistry, geology, and biology. The evolutionary theory stands in opposition to the Bible and to the facts of paleontology and biology. The ideas of young-earth creationists are not supported by God's Word either, conflicting with astronomy, physics, and geology.

Back in the seventeenth century, the world-renowned scientist Galileo proved beyond any doubt that the earth was not the center of the universe, nor did the sun orbit the earth. In fact, he proved it to be the other way around (no pun intended), with the earth revolving around the sun. However, he was brought up on charges of heresy by the Roman Catholic Church and ordered to recant his position. Why? From the viewpoint of the Catholic Church, Galileo was contradicting God's Word, the Bible. As it turned out, Galileo and science were correct and the Church was wrong, for which it issued a formal apology in 1992. However, the point we wish to make here is that in all the controversy, the Bible was never in the wrong. It was a misinterpretation on the part of the Catholic Church, and not a fault with the Bible. One will find no place in the Bible that claims the sun orbits the earth. So where would the Church get such an idea? From Ptolemy (b. about 85 C.E.), an ancient astronomer, who argued for such an idea.

This geocentric model that the earth is the center of the universe was long held by Ptolemy's predecessors like Aristotle and most of the ancient Greek philosophers. The idea of the earth being the center of the universe was held on to by the fact that the observer with his naked eye saw both the sun and moon appear to revolve around the earth each day, while the earth appeared to stand still. Now consider that the church fathers of the third to the fifth centuries C.E. were inundated by Greek thought, believing philosophical thinking was a means of interpreting God's Word. Commenting on such ones, Douglas T. Holden[61] stated, "Christian theology has become so fused with Greek philosophy that it has reared individuals who are a mixture of nine parts Greek thought to one part Christian thought." Couple this with a literal reading of some texts that should be understood figuratively and you have the makings for a conflict between the Church and the scientific world.

In interpretation, you may find one verse that appears to be in direct conflict with another (such as, the earth will be destroyed by fire, or, the earth will last forever). We do not automatically assume that God's original Word is wrong. We must do some investigative work. (1) Is there a scribal error? (2) Is there an error in translation? (3) Is this a case of one verse using "earth" in a literal sense, while another is using figurative language, speaking of mankind as the "earth?" This can be the case with science as well. One does not let the scientific world dictate our understanding of Scripture, but we should not be so dogmatic in the face of scientific facts that we will, like Professor Kirk Wise, set aside "all the evidence in the universe [that] turns against creationism," while still holding onto erroneous, unreasonable, and unscriptural interpretations.

We have many of conservative scholarship who still argue that the earth and all life on it were created in six literal 24-hour days. As you may know, this flatly contradicts

---

[61] Douglas T. Holden, *Death Shall Have no Dominion: A New Testament Study* (Bloomington: Bethany Press, 1971), 14.

modern-day science. Do we have another Galileo moment in time? Who is correct here, the scholars or science? One thing is for certain; there is no fault to be found in God's Word. The Bible does not explicitly say these creative days were literal 24-hour days. What many are failing to realize and quite a few refuse to accept is that, in both the Hebrew and the Greek Scriptures, the word for "day" (Heb., yohm; Gr., hemera) is used both in a literal and in a figurative sense. Moreover, this is not a case of inerrancy. In other words, if one does not accept six literal 24-hour days, he has abandoned inerrancy. True inerrancy does not consider whether they are literal or figurative creative days, but rather is your interpretation in harmony with what the author meant by the words that he used.

These six creative days are representative of being like six successive days of a week. If we look at most modern translations, they read, "**the** first day," "**the** second day," "**the** third day," and so on. This is an error in translation and should read. "And there was evening and there was morning, **a** first day." (Gen. 1:5) There is no definite article in the Hebrew of these six creative days. It is the translators that choose to add it into their translations. (ESV, LEB, HCSB, NIV, etc.) However, the American Standard Version and the New American Standard Bible read, "And there was evening and there was morning, one day." (1:5) If we were talking about a definite period of time, generally there should be a definite article in the Hebrew, because it is written in the prose genre. It is only in Hebrew poetry that the definite article could be omitted. What we are looking at with these six creative days is simply a sequential pattern, as oppose to six literal units of definite time.

SIX CREATIVE DAYS		
Day	**Works**	**Genesis**
1	Light gradually came to be;[62] a separation between day and night	1:3–5
2	Expanse, a separation between the waters below from the waters above	1:6–8
3	Dry land appears; produces vegetation	1:9–13
4	Sources of light now become visible from earth[63]	1:14–19
5	Aquatic souls and flying creatures	1:20–23
6	Land animals; man and woman created	1:24–31

---

[62] Many believe that God said, "Let there be light" and it immediately appeared. No, this was a gradual process, taking such an enormous amount of time that speculation would be the result of any guess. J. W. Watt's translation reflects this gradual process: "And gradually light came into existence." (A Distinctive Translation of Genesis) This light from our sun was spread through the dark overcast, to the point that it was not at first observable but gradually became observable through time.

[63] And God said, "Let there be light," and there was light, the first day. Hebrew has different words that distinguish their source and their quality. The Hebrew word used in verse one for "light" is ohr, which carries the general sense. However, by the fourth "day," or creative period, the Hebrew word changes to maohr, which is now referring to the source of the light.

While the word "day" in Hebrew can mean a 24-hour period, clearly *yohm* and its context allows the creative days to be understood as a period of time, an age, or an era. For example, immediately after he mentions the six creative days, Moses uses the same word for "day" in a more general way, lumping *all six creative days together as one day*:

Genesis 2:4: These are the generations of the heavens and of the earth when they were created, in the day that Jehovah God made earth and heaven.

Here we are given the context of just how Moses is using *yohm*, which in this verse is referring to all six creative periods as "in the day." With this alone, it is difficult to argue that in chapter one *yohm* was being used to refer literally to a 24-hour period. Below are a few other examples where *yohm* is being used in the sense of an extended period of time, age, or era:

Proverbs 25:13 (HCSB): a trustworthy messenger is like the coolness of snow on *a harvest day* [*yohm*]; he refreshes the life of his masters.

Proverbs 25:13 (NASB): Like the cold of snow in the time [*yohm*, ftn lit. day] of harvest, Is a faithful messenger to those who send him, For he refreshes the soul of his masters.

Isaiah 4:2 (ASV): *In that day* [*yohm*] shall the branch of Jehovah be beautiful and glorious, and the fruit of the land shall be excellent and comely for them that are escaped of Israel.

Zechariah 14:1 (ASV): Behold, *a day* [*yohm*] *of* Jehovah cometh, when thy spoil shall be divided in the midst of thee.

You will have those who cling to the 24-hour creative day by informing you that *yohm*, "day," is used 410 times outside of Genesis with a day and number and in all cases it is to be taken literally, meaning an ordinary day. First, let us point out that there is no absolute grammatical rule in Hebrew that would make this mandatory in every case. Young-earth proponents must support their proposition with their circular argument. For the sake of an argument, let us say that their claim is true. To have "day" used with an ordinal number in 410 places outside of Genesis chapter one would not negate *yohm* being used in a different setting (like creation) with ordinal numbers and still be referring to periods of time (epochs). One must keep in mind that those uses of a *yohm* outside the creation account are used in reference to humans and a human day. Because Genesis is the only place in Scripture where periods of time can be used with ordinal numbers, there is no problem with it being the exception to the rule. No other book has the setting of the creation of heaven and earth, so to equate uses of *yohm* in totally different settings with its use in Genesis is circular reasoning, as if to say: "*Yohm* is used with ordinals in 410 occurrences outside of Genesis and they are literal, so *yohm* must be literal in Genesis because it is used with ordinal numbers." You might as well say that "*yohm* is literal with ordinal numbers because *yohm* should be literal with ordinal numbers." The young-earth proponent's argument is circular by supporting a premise with a premise instead of a conclusion.

Exodus 20:11 (ASV): For in six days Jehovah made heaven and earth, the sea, and all that in them is, and rested the seventh day: wherefore Jehovah blessed the sabbath day, and hallowed it.

Is Moses, the writer of Genesis, making reference here at Exodus 20:11 to the six creative days as a representative for the weekly Sabbath, thus suggesting that the six creative days were literal 24-hour days? No, this is not so. At Genesis 2:4, the same writer uses *yohm*, "day," figuratively to refer to the six creative days of Genesis chapter one and Exodus 20:11 as a whole, starting from the gradual appearance of light on the first day (Genesis 1:3 as it would appear to an earthly observer), but does not include the earth as it lay in its prior existence, in which it is described as being "without form and void, and darkness was over the face of the deep. And the Spirit of God was hovering over the face of the waters."

Another obstacle for those who wish to take the creation account in a literal sense of 24-hour periods is that the context is really presented as events that take long periods of time to accomplish.

Genesis 1:11, 12 (ASV): And God said, Let the earth put forth grass, herbs yielding seed, and fruit-trees bearing fruit after their kind, wherein is the seed thereof, upon the earth: and it was so. [Resulting in] And the earth brought forth grass, herbs yielding seed after their kind, and trees bearing fruit, wherein is the seed thereof, after their kind: and God saw that it was good.

Obviously we are dealing with far more time than one 24-hour day would allow when speaking of grass, herbs, and fruit trees sprouting *and* growing to maturity *and* producing seed and fruit.

Genesis 2:18–20 (ASV): And Jehovah God said, It is not good *that the man should be alone;* I will make him a help meet for him. And out of the ground Jehovah God formed every beast of the field, and every bird of the heavens; and brought them unto the man to see what he would call them: and whatsoever the man called every living creature, that was the name thereof. And the man gave names to all cattle, and to the birds of the heavens, and to every beast of the field; but for man there was not found a help meet for him.

At this point in the creation account it was still the sixth creative day. However as verse 27 of chapter 1 shows, it is the close of the sixth creation day. After all else had been created, after the animals had been fashioned, just before sundown of that day, "God created man in his own image, in the image of God he created him; male and female he created them." Taken literally, this means that Adam and Eve were created in the last hour of the sixth day. The question here is, if the sixth "day" was only going to be 24 hours, why would Adam be lonely? God would have known he was creating his helper in that sixth "day." Why the concern for loneliness if it were only moments before Eve was to be created? For this reader, the implication is that the sixth day is a long creative period.

Even more activity would be impossibly crammed into the sixth creative day if it were only a 24-hour period. Adam is assigned the task of naming the different kinds of animals. This is not a simple task of just picking a name randomly. In the ancient culture, names carried even more meaning than in our modern Western culture. Names were chosen to be descriptive, to reflect something about the person, animal, or thing. From the descriptive forms of the names Adam chose, it is obvious that it took some time, for the account literally reads, "whatever the man called *every living creature*, that was its name."[64] (Genesis 2:19) For example, the Hebrew word for the "ass" refers to the usual reddened color. The

---

[64] Walter A. Elwell and Barry J Beitzel, *Baker Encyclopedia of the Bible* (Grand Rapids, Mich.: Baker Book House, 1988), S. 93.

Hebrew word for stork is the feminine form of the word meaning "loyal one."[65] This name is certainly a perfect fit, as the stork is known for the loving care it gives its young, and the loyalty of staying with its mate for life, something that would have been impossible to observe within a mere 24-hour day.

Regardless, it has been estimated, even if Adam has taken just one minute to name each pair, it would have taken 40 days with no sleep. It was only after Adam completed this task that Eve was created. Yet, even conceding the possibility that the process of naming the animals went quicker, because Adam named only the basic kinds of animals, like what went in Noah's ark at the time of the flood, which did not involve thousands of creatures, it would have taken weeks, possibly months, not a literal 24-hour day. It is during the process of Adam's naming the animals that it is discovered that "for the man no helper was found who was like him." (Genesis 2:20) Thus, we now see where the concern from Genesis 2:18 comes from, with God's reference to Adam's getting lonely. If it took weeks, months, or decades for Adam to complete his assignment of naming the animals, he would have had the time to grow lonely, but not in a couple hours as would be the case with a 24-hour day. Thus, the context here is that over a long period of time of naming the animals, Adam took note that he was alone while all the animals had mates. Let us take an extensive look at this again with the leading Hebrew language scholar of the 20th century, Dr. Gleason L. Archer.

---

[65] *Enhanced Brown-Driver-Briggs Hebrew and English Lexicon.* electronic ed. (Oak Harbor, WA : Logos Research Systems, 2000), S. 339.

It thus becomes clear in this present case, as we study the text of Genesis 1, that we must not short-circuit our responsibility of careful exegesis in order to ascertain as clearly as possible what the divine author meant by the language His inspired prophet (in this case probably Moses) was guided to employ. Is the true purpose of Genesis 1 to teach that all creation began just six twenty-four-hour days before Adam was "born"? Or is this just a mistaken inference that overlooks other biblical data having a direct bearing on this passage? To answer this question we must take careful note of what is said in Genesis 1:27 concerning the creation of man as the closing act of the sixth creative day. There it is stated that on that sixth day (apparently toward the end of the day, after all the animals had been fashioned and placed on the earth—therefore not long before sundown at the end of that same day), "God created man in His own image; He created them male and female." This can only mean that Eve was created in the closing hour of Day Six, along with Adam.

As we turn to Genesis 2, however, we find that a considerable interval of time must have intervened between the creation of Adam and the creation of Eve. In Gen. 2:15 we are told that Yahweh Elohim (i.e., the LORD God) put Adam in the garden of Eden as the idle environment for his development, and there he was to cultivate and keep the enormous park, with all its goodly trees, abundant fruit crop, and four mighty rivers that flowed from Eden to other regions of the Near East. In Gen 2:18 we read, "Then the LORD God said, 'It is not good for the man to be alone; I will make him a helper suitable for him.' " This statement clearly implies that Adam had been diligently occupied in his responsible task of pruning, harvesting fruit, and keeping the ground free of brush and undergrowth for a long enough period to lose his initial excitement and sense of thrill at this wonderful occupation in the beautiful paradise of Eden. He had begun to feel a certain lonesomeness and inward dissatisfaction.

In order to compensate for this lonesomeness, God then gave Adam a major assignment in natural history. He was to classify every species of animal and bird found in the preserve. With its five mighty rivers and broad expanse, the garden must have had hundreds of species of mammal, reptile, insect, and bird, to say nothing of the flying insects that also are indicated by the basic Hebrew term 'ôp̱ ("bird") (2:19). It took the Swedish scientist Linnaeus several decades to classify all the species known to European scientists in the eighteenth century. Doubtless there were considerably more by that time than in Adam's day; and, of course, the range of fauna in Eden may have been more limited than those available to Linnaeus. But at the same time it must have taken a good deal of study for Adam to examine each specimen and decide on an appropriate name for it, especially in view of the fact that he had absolutely no human tradition behind him, so far as nomenclature was concerned. It must have required some years, or, at the very least, a considerable number of months for him to complete this comprehensive inventory of all the birds, beasts, and insects that populated the Garden of Eden.

Finally, after this assignment with all its absorbing interest had been completed, Adam felt a renewed sense of emptiness. Genesis 2:20 ends with the words "but for Adam no suitable helper was found." After this long and unsatisfying experience as a lonely bachelor, God saw that Adam was emotionally prepared for a wife—a "suitable helper." God, therefore, subjected him to a deep sleep, removed from his body the bone that was closest to his heart, and from that physical core of man fashioned the first woman. Finally God presented woman to Adam in all her fresh, unspoiled beauty, and Adam was ecstatic with joy.

As we have compared Scripture with Scripture (Gen. 1:27 with 2:15–22), it has become very apparent that Genesis 1 was never intended to teach that the sixth creative day, when Adam and Eve were both created, lasted a mere twenty-four hours. In view of the long interval of time between these two, it would seem to border on sheer irrationality to insist that all of Adam's experiences in Genesis 2:15–22 could have been crowded into the last hour or two of a literal twenty-four-hour day. The only reasonable conclusion to draw is that the purpose of Genesis 1 is not to tell how fast God performed His work of creation (though, of course, some of His acts, such as the creation of light on the first day, must have been instantaneous). Rather, its true purpose was to reveal that the Lord God who had revealed Himself to the Hebrew race and entered into personal covenant relationship with them was indeed the only true God, the Creator of all things that are. This stood in direct opposition to the religious notions of the heathen around them, who assumed the emergence of pantheon of gods in successive stages out of preexistent matter of unknown origin, actuated by forces for which there was no accounting.[66]

Below, we see more examples of accounts within creation that are not instantaneous.

Genesis 2:8-9 American Standard Version (ASV)

⁸ And Jehovah God planted a garden in Eden, in the East, and there he put the man whom he had formed. ⁹ And **out of the ground made Jehovah God to grow every tree** that is pleasant to the sight, and good for food; the tree of life also in the midst of the garden, and the tree of the knowledge of good and evil.

The straightforward reading of this text is that it is not an instantaneous creation. It is that Jehovah God planted the trees, and they grew as we understand trees grow, in a normal fashion.

Genesis 1:11-12 English Standard Version (ESV)

11 And God said, "Let the earth sprout vegetation, plants yielding seed, and fruit trees bearing fruit in which is their seed, each according to its kind, on the earth." And it was so. **12** The earth **brought forth vegetation**, plants yielding seed

---

[66] Gleason L. Archer, New International Encyclopedia of Bible Difficulties, Zondervan's Understand the Bible Reference Series, 59-60 (Grand Rapids, MI: Zondervan Publishing House, 1982).

according to their own kinds, and trees bearing fruit in which is their seed, each according to its kind. And God saw that it was good.

Here again, the straightforward reading, we are seeing the natural process of all vegetation, as opposed to it being created instantly.

In addition, it should be noted that God's Word explicitly helps man to appreciate that a "day" to Jehovah God is not measured in the same way as man's.

Psalm 90:4 (AS): For in Your sight a thousand years are like yesterday that passes by, like a few hours of the night.

2 Peter 3:8 (ASV): Dear friends, don't let this one thing escape you: with the Lord one day is like 1,000 years, and 1,000 years like one day.

2 Peter 3:10 (ASV): But the Day of the Lord will come like a thief; on that [day] the heavens will pass away with a loud noise, the elements will burn and be dissolved, and the earth and the works on it will be disclosed.

Going Back to the Beginning

Genesis 1:1 English Standard Version (ESV)

¹ **In the beginning**, God created the heavens and the earth.

What do we learn from this one little phrase? **First**, the universe had a beginning. **Second**, since Jehovah God is the Creator of the Universe, then his existence is outside of creation, In other words, God is existing outside the material universe and so not limited by it. He is beyond, outside of his creation. **Third**, prior to the creation account of the universe, there was no matter and energy. Rather, the universe was created from nothing. **Fourth**, before Genesis 1:1 activity, there was no time as we know it. **Fifth**, God is the sovereign of the universe, and it is him alone that sets the laws and standards that exist under the umbrella of that sovereignty. The 24 elders on the Revelation of John proclaim, "Worthy are you, our Lord and God, to receive glory and honor and power, for you created all things, and by your will they existed and were created." (Rev. 4:11) It is beyond science as to how matter and energy came into existence, because what they do know by natural law (thermodynamics), 'energy cannot be created or destroyed.' All science can do is accept the matter and energy are givens. On the other hand, God's Word is clear that he supernaturally created matter, energy, space, and time as well as the laws that govern them.

Genesis 1:2 English Standard Version (ESV)

² The earth was without form and void, and darkness was over the face of the deep. And the Spirit of God was hovering over the face of the waters.

In order to deal with the scientific view that the universe is 20 billion years old, they would postulate that that time is to be found between Genesis 1:1 and 1:2. This is why in some translations, you find a space between verse 1 and verse 2, which is known as the Gap Theory (or Restitution Theory).[67]

---

[67] This is "as if some great catastrophe (presumably the fall of Satan and his banishment to Earth) befell Earth after its original perfect and complete creation. On this view the six days of creation actually represent the re-creation of the world after its original demise. This view is not widely supported today because it is neither consistent with the grammar of the text nor supportable from the scientific evidence. Nonetheless, it is impossible to know how much (if any) time elapsed between verses 1 and 2." (Whorton 2008)

There is no reason to suggest such an idea, it is simply that God by way of his human author, Moses, informed the readers of the creation of the universe, followed by the condition of the earth, before God turn his attention to carrying out acts of creation on the earth, to prepare it for human habitation. According to verses 1 and 2, the universe, which includes the earth was in existence for an unknown period of time before God began the creative days.

First Day: Light (1:3–5)

Genesis 1:3-5 Updated American Standard Version (UASV)

³And God proceeded to say, "Let light come to be, and there came to be light. ⁴ And God saw that the light was good. And God divided the light from the darkness. ⁵ God began calling the light Day, and the darkness he called Night. And there came to be evening and there came to be morning, one day.

There are many different interpretations about how long the Genesis creation days were. We are only going to concern ourselves with two, because one is the orthodox position, the other is the second most common position and the position of the author. For a discussion of the length of the Genesis day, please see the first difficulty in the Bible Difficulties in Genesis, Genesis 1:1 Is the earth only 6,000 to 10,000 years old? Are the creative days literally, only 24 hours long? Keep in mind that a different interpretation of this does not alter the inerrancy of Scripture, because it is an interpretation of Scripture, not an error in Scripture. Also, you can listen to the evidence, and make the decision for yourself.

When we look at verses 2-5 of Genesis chapter 1, we need to appreciate that this is not the birth of the sun and the moon; they were there in outer space long before that first creative day. However, they would not have been visible until this time, if one were on the earth. Now, on this first creative day, light evidently punched through the expanse that surrounded the earth, so that it would have been visible to an earthly observer, had there been one. Thus, there was now an evening and there was morning, the first day, because of the rotating earth.

Second Day: The Expanse (1:6–8)

Genesis 1:6-8 English Standard Version (ESV)

⁶ And God said, "Let there be an expanse in the midst of the waters, and let it separate the waters from the waters." ⁷ And God made the expanse and separated the waters that were under the expanse from the waters that were above the expanse. And it was so. ⁸ And God called the expanse Heaven. And there was evening and there was morning, the second day.

Some older translations like the King James Version and the American Standard Version reads "let there be a firmament." Modern translations read like the ESV above, "let there be an expanse." Bible critics tried to use the rendering "firmament" to say that the Bible writers borrowed from the creation myths, as some are picture with this "firmament" as a metal dome. However, even within the King James Version, the marginal reading is "expanse." The Hebrew word, raqia, for "expanse" means "to spread out, stamp, or expand."

We do not understand how the Almighty God bright this separation about, pushing the waters up from the earth, until the circle of the earth was surrounded by "waters that were above the expanse." Genesis 1:20 reads "let birds fly above the earth across the expanse of the heavens."

What took place on the second "day"? How have Bible critics tried to us the poor translation of the Hebrew word for "expanse"? What picture can you draw in your mind as God accomplished the separation of the waters from the waters?

Third Day (a): Land (1:9–10)

Genesis 1:9-10 English Standard Version (ESV)

⁹ And God said, "Let the waters under the heavens be gathered together into one place, and let the dry land appear." And it was so. ¹⁰ God called the dry land Earth, and the waters that were gathered together he called Seas. And God saw that it was good.

Again, we should not expect Moses to disclose explicit detail as to how this was accomplished. However, we can see the exercise of great power on the part of God, as we are being informed about incredible earth movements in the formation of land areas. The geologist, who studies the structure of the earth, would see verses 9-10 as a series of sudden violent catastrophes. Moses, on the other hand, indicates clear direction and control by our Creator, as he formed the earth to be inhabited.

In the book of Job, He questions God. Therefore, God takes Job to task over the creation account, by asking Job numerous questions that emphasizes the greatness of God over against man. Where was Job when the earth was created? Can job measure the earth? How is it that the earth just hangs in the sky?

Job 38:3-6 English Standard Version (ESV)

³ Dress for action like a man;
  I will question you, and you make it known to me.

⁴ "Where were you when I laid the foundation of the earth?
  Tell me, if you have understanding.
⁵ Who determined its measurements—surely you know!
  Or who stretched the line upon it?
⁶ On what were its bases sunk,
  or who laid its cornerstone,

Third Day (b): Vegetation (1:11-13)

Genesis 1:11 English Standard Version (ESV)

¹¹ And God said, "Let the earth sprout vegetation, plants, yielding seed, and fruit trees bearing fruit in which is their seed, each according to its kind, on the earth." And it was so.

The light from the sun was now coming through the expanse much stronger by this time, to the point of photosynthesis, which is an absolute need to green plants. This is the process by which green plants and other organisms turn carbon dioxide and water into carbohydrates and oxygen, using light energy trapped by chlorophyll.

Fourth Day: Sun, Moon, and Stars, (1:14–19)

Genesis 1:3, 5 English Standard Version (ESV)

³And God said, "**Let there be light**," and there was light. ⁵And there was evening and there was morning, **the first day**.

Genesis 1:16, 19 English Standard Version (ESV)

¹⁶And **God made the two great lights**—the greater light to rule the day and the lesser light to rule the night—and the stars. ¹⁹And there was evening and there was morning, **the fourth day**.

In the above there appears to be a Bible difficulty, in that Genesis 1:3, 5 informs the reader that God brought about light during the first creation day, when he said: "'Let there be light,' and there was light." Then, Genesis 1:16, 19 informs the reader that "God made the two great lights" during the fourth creation day. Hence, did God create or make light on the first or fourth creation day? Before we begin to answer this difficulty, we must bear in mind that Genesis was written from a human perspective, as an earthly observer, as if he were there; not from a heavenly observation.

In looking at the fourth creation day first, we see that the "greater light" for ruling the day is our sun, and the "lesser light" for ruling the night is our moon. A further explanation of this is found at Psalm 136:7-9 (ASV): "To him that made great lights; for his loving-kindness endures forever: The sun to rule by day; for his loving-kindness endures forever; the moon and stars to rule by night; for his loving-kindness endures forever."

Returning to the first creation day, we find the expression: "let there be light." *Ohr* is the Hebrew word for light, which conveys the idea of light in a broad sense. However, for the fourth creation day, a different word is chosen, *maohr*, which refers to a source of light. Rotherham, in a footnote on "Luminaries" in the *Emphasised Bible*, says: "In ver. 3, 'ôr [*ohr*], light diffused." Then he goes on to show that the Hebrew word *maohr* in verse 14 has the sense of something "affording light." In other words, on the first creation day *ohr* (light) was spread throughout the earth's atmosphere (being diffused). To an earthly observer, had he been there: he would have not been able to discern the source of light. However, by the fourth creation day, the observer would have been able to see the *maohr* (source) of that light, as the atmosphere would have changed.

It should also be noted that Genesis 1:16 does not use the Hebrew verb bara, meaning, "create." Instead, the Hebrew verb asah is used, meaning, "make." The reason being, Genesis 1:1 informs us "God created the heavens (which would include sun, moon and stars) and the earth." In other words, the "greater light" (sun) and the "lesser light" (moon) were created long before the fourth creation day. What we have on the fourth creation day is Jehovah God "making" the "greater light" and the "lesser light" to exist in a new way with the surface of the earth and the expanse that had now dissipated even further, allowing the source of light to be seen from earth. God said, "Let there be lights in the expanse of the heavens . . ." (Gen 1:14). This being a further indication of their discernibleness. In addition, they were "to separate the day from the night. And let them be for signs and for seasons, and for days and years." These were to evidence the existence of God and draw attention to His great power, as well as lead man in numerous ways.

Those who steadfastly argue for the young earth view in light of all the evidence against the, here again, this creates a problem, because they also argue that the earth's sun was not created until the fourth day, it literally did not exist until the fourth day. Some suggest that the light from the first creation day was not from our sun but from another source, maybe a temporary light source, or the illumination of God himself. The problem with this, there literal 24 hour days for the first three days had solar days, because they see the text "there was evening and there was morning" as literal. How do you have solar days for three creation days, without our sun? If these three creative days are not defined by our sun, then the length of those days are unclear. As you can see, this is just another monumental difficulty for those that would take the creation account to be literal, when it was not meant to be taken that way.

Fifth Day: Sea Animals and Birds, (1:20–25)

Genesis 1:20-21 English Standard Version (ESV)

²⁰ And God said, "Let the waters swarm with swarms of living creatures [souls],[68] and let birds fly above the earth across the expanse of the heavens." ²¹ So God created the great sea creatures and every living creature [soul] that moves, with which the waters swarm, according to their kinds, and every winged bird according to its kind. And God saw that it was good.

The literal translations here decided to be a little more dynamic equivalent in their rendering of the Hebrew nephesh chaiyah, living soul. The term applies to the creatures in the sea, as well as the birds 'flying above the earth across the expanse of the heavens.' This would also apply to the fossil remains of sea monsters that have been discovered in recent

---

[68] Heb., nephesh chaiyah, singular, "living soul"

times. If we are to fully understand the soul, it would be best to render the Hebrew nephesh (soul) and the Greek Psyche (soul) literally.

Sixth Day: Land Animals and Man, (1:24–31)

Genesis 1:24-31 Lexham English Bible (LEB)

[24] And God said, "Let the earth bring forth living creatures according to their kind: cattle and moving things, and wild animals according to their kind." And it was so. [25] So God made wild animals according to their kind and the cattle according to their kind, and every creeping thing of the earth according to its kind. And God saw that *it was* good.

[26] And God said, "Let us make humankind in our image and according to our likeness, and let them rule over the fish of the sea, and over the birds of heaven, and over the cattle, and over all the earth, and over every moving thing that moves upon the earth." [27] So God created humankind in his image, in the likeness of God he created him, male and female he created them. [28] And God blessed them, and God said to them, "Be fruitful and multiply, and fill the earth and subdue it, and rule over the fish of the sea and the birds of heaven,]and over every animal that moves upon the earth."

[29] And God said, "Look—I am giving to you every plant *that* bears seed which *is* on the face of the whole earth, and every kind of tree *that bears fruit*. They shall be yours as food." [30] And to every kind of animal of the earth and to every bird of heaven, and to everything that moves upon the earth in which *there is* life *I am giving* every green plant as food." And it was so. [31] And God saw everything that he had made and, behold, *it was* very good. And there was evening, and there was morning, a sixth day.

As you can see on the sixth creation day we are introduced to the creation of both domestic and wild animals, these being in relation to what man could tame and use domestically, as opposed to what remain wild. Within this creation period was also the greatest of all creation, the creation of both man and woman. It with the creation of humans alone that it was said they were 'created in the image of God.'

Then there is the problem of the seventh day, as far as the young earth view is concerned: it never ended. There was no opening and closing, as occurred with the preceding six days; it is still in progress from the close of the sixth day, more than 6,000 years ago.

Hebrews 4:4, 5, 9–11 (ASV): For somewhere He has spoken about the seventh day in this way: And on the seventh day God rested from all His works. Again, in that passage [He says], They will never enter My rest. A Sabbath rest remains, therefore, for God's people. For the person who has entered His rest has rested from his own works, just as God did from His. Let us then make every effort to enter that rest, so that no one will fall into the same pattern of disobedience.

Clearly, the context of God's Word as a whole shows the earth to be much older than 6,000+ years.

Habakkuk 3:6 (ASV): He stood, and measured the earth; He beheld, and drove asunder the nations; And the *eternal mountains* were scattered; The *everlasting hills* did bow; His goings were as of old.

Micah 6:2 (ASV): Hear, O ye mountains, Jehovah's controversy, and ye *enduring foundations of the earth*; for

Jehovah hath a controversy with his people, and he will contend with Israel.

Proverbs 8:22, 23 (ASV): Jehovah possessed me in the beginning of his way, Before his works of old. I was set up from everlasting, from the beginning, Before the earth was.

The writer of Proverbs is using the age of the earth to emphasize that wisdom is much older. But if one accepts the young-earth theory (4004 B.C.E. for the creation of man),[69] when Solomon, who died shortly after 1000 B.C.E., wrote this, the earth would have been only about 3,000 years old—so not much of an emphasis.

Science has established that light travels at 186,282 miles per second. We know that it takes 100,000 years for light to cross our galaxy. We also know that it has taken hundreds of millions of years for the light of the stars we now see to reach the earth. Let us not repeat the Galileo history once more. It takes humility to learn from past experience. The Galileo conflict between science and the Church should at the very least help dogmatic conservative scholarship to avoid taking "day" as a literal 24-hour day when Scripture itself allows for another understanding; context weighs in that direction and science has established that the earth and the universe are far older than 6,000–10,000 years. Regardless of whether some scholars will concede to the correct understanding, this would in no way put the Bible in the wrong, for it is its interpreters who have misunderstood it. We must keep in mind that science (or the scientist) has no quarrel with the Bible: the

---

[69] Archbishop James Usher (1581–1656) developed a chronology of the Bible, and dated creation at 4004 B.C.E.

quarrel would be with the misinterpretation of the teachers of Christendom, orthodox Jews, and others.

The website ChristianAnswers.Net concludes: "The lesson to be learned from Galileo, it appears, is not that the Church held too tightly to biblical truths; but rather that it did not hold tightly enough. It allowed Greek philosophy to influence its theology and held to tradition rather than to the teachings of the Bible. We must hold strongly to Biblical doctrine which has been achieved through sure methods of exegesis. We must never be satisfied with dogmas built upon philosophic traditions."[70] However, it is also true that science alone should not determine our interpretation, but it is to be used in a balanced way, as another source to consider.

The Copernican theory was, in fact, condemned by the theologians of the Inquisition and Pope Urban VIII. They argued that it contradicted the Bible: to be specific, Joshua's statement: "O sun, stand still . . . So the sun stood still, and the moon stopped." (Joshua 10:12, ESV) Of course, this is not meant to be taken literally. There are several reasonable explanations, one of which, I will give you here. Verse 13 says that "the sun stopped in the midst of heaven and did not hurry to set for about a whole day." This could simply allow for a slower movement of the earth, giving the appearance to an earthly observer that the sun and moon had stood still. As for another reasonable explanation, one Bible encyclopedia comments: "While this could mean a stopping of earth's rotation, it could have been accomplished by other means, such as a refraction of solar and lunar light rays to produce

---

[70] http://www.christiananswers.net/q-eden/edn-c007.html. (Accessed January 28, 2010.)

the same effect." Therefore, once more, it becomes obvious that the Bible does not contradict itself.

In Summary

The Hebrew word for day that was used for the creation days of Genesis chapter 1 is the same word used at Genesis 2:4 as a reference to the whole of the creative period, six days, "in the day that . . ."

The Bible uses the word for "day" as longer periods than a 24-hour day "one day is as a thousand years." (2 Peter 3:8; Psalm 90:4)

There are indicators within the first two chapters that we are dealing with periods longer than 24-hour days.

(1) **Third Day**: At Genesis 1:11-12, we find that trees grew from seeds to maturity, and produced seeds of their kind. This takes months, even years.

(2) **Sixth day**: We find Adam was created, went to sleep, named thousands of animals (names that indicate observation of the animals), grew lonely (looking for a helper), went to sleep, Eve was produced out of Adam's rib. This is obviously longer than 24 hours.

(3) **Seventh Day**: Genesis 2:2 informs us that God "proceeded to rest."[71] The reader will note that Hebrews 4:4 shows that God is still in His rest from the ending of the six creative days. Therefore, the seventh day has been running for thousands of years thus far, which allows the other creative days to be thousands of years long.

---

[71] * Why do I have it rendered as a continuous, "proceeded to rest", when most translations read "he rested"? Heb., waiyishboth (imperfect sequential): The verb is in the imperfect state denoting incomplete or continuous action, or action in progress.

As it usually turns out, the so-called contradiction between science and God's Word lies at the feet of those who are interpreting Scripture incorrectly. To repeat the sentiments of Galileo when writing to a pupil—Galileo expressed the same sentiments: "Even though Scripture cannot err, its interpreters and expositors can, in various ways. One of these, very serious and very frequent, would be when they always want to stop at the purely literal sense."[72] I believe that today's scholars, in hindsight, would have no problem agreeing.

Procedures for Handling Biblical Difficulties

1. You need to be completely convinced a reason or understanding exists.

2. You need to have total trust and conviction in the inerrancy of the Scripture as originally written down.

3. You need to study the context and framework of the verse carefully, to establish what the author meant by the words he used. In other words, find the beginning and the end of the context that your passage falls within.

4. You need to understand exegesis: find the historical setting, determine author intent, study key words, and note parallel passages. You need to slow down and carefully read the account, considering exactly what is being said

5. You need to find a reasonable harmonization of parallel passages.

---

[72] Letter from Galileo to Benedetto Castelli, December 21, 1613.

6. You need to consider a variety of trusted Bible commentaries, dictionaries, lexical sources, encyclopedias, as well as books on Bible difficulties.

7. You should investigate as to whether the difficulty is a transmissional error in the original text.

8. You must always keep in mind that the historical accuracy of the biblical text is unmatched; that thousands of extant manuscripts some of which date back to the second century B.C. support the transmitted text of Scripture.

9. We must keep in mind that the Bible is a diverse book when it comes to literary styles: narrative, poetic, prophetic, and apocalyptic; also containing parables, metaphors, similes, hyperbole, and other figures of speech. Too often, these alleged errors are the result of a reader taking a figure of speech as literal, or reading a parable as though it is a narrative.

10. The Bible student needs to understand what level that the Bible intends to be exact in what is written. If Jim told a friend that 650 graduated with him from high school in 1984, it is not challenged, because it is all too clear that he is using rounded numbers and is not meaning to be precise.[73]

---

[73] If you enjoyed this APPENDIX E, please see, *IS THE BIBLE REALLY THE WORD OF GOD?: Myths? Errors? Contradictions? Scientifically Inaccurate? by Andrews, Edward D. (Feb 17, 2014)*

http://www.christianpublishers.org/apps/webstore/products/show/4676333

Bibliography

Adsit, B. Christopher. *Personal Disciple-Making.* San Bernardino, CA: Here's Life Publishers, Inc., 1988.

Aldrich, C Joseph. *Lifestyle Evangelism.* Portland, OR: Multnoma Press, 1981.

Andrews, Edward D. *THE EVANGELISM HANDBOOK: How All Christians Can Effectively Share God's Word in Their Community.* Cambridge: Christian Publishing House, 2013.

Archer, Gleason L. *Encyclopedia of Bible Difficulties.* Grand Rapids: Zondervan, 1982.

Arndt, William, Frederick W. Danker, and Walter Bauer. *A Greek-English Lexicon of the New Testament and Other Early Christian Literature.* 3rd ed. . Chicago: University of Chicago Press, 2000.

Barna, George. *Marketing the Church.* Carol Stream, IL: Navepress, 1988.

Boa, Kenneth, and Kruidenier. *Holman New Testament Commentary: Romans.* Nashville: Broadman & Holman, 2000.

Boyd, Gregory A, and Paul R Eddy. *Across the Spectrum.* Grand Rapids: Baker Academic, 2002.

Brand, Chad, Charles Draper, and England Archie. *Holman Illustrated Bible Dictionary: Revised, Updated and Expanded.* Nashville, TN: Holman, 2003.

Brown, Francis, Samuel Rolles Driver, and Charles Augustus Briggs. *Enhanced Brown-Driver-Briggs Hebrew and*

English Lexicon . Oak Harbor: Logos Research Systems, 2000.

Campbell, Barry. *Smaller Churches Healthy and Growing.* Nashville, TN: LifeWay Press, 1998.

Coleman, E. Robert. *The Master Plan of Evangelism.* Westwood, NJ: Fleming H. Revell Company, 1964.

Comfort, Philip. *Encountering the Manuscripts: An Introduction to New Testament Paleography and Textual Criticism.* Nashville: Broadman & Holman, 2005.

Dallas, Willard. *The Spirit of the Disciplines.* San Francisco: Harper/Collins, 1988.

Dever, Mark. *Nine Marks of a Healthy Church.* Wheaton, IL: Crossway Books, 2000.

Eckman, James P. *Exploring Church History* . Wheaton, Ill: Crossway, 2002.

Eims, LeRoy. *One to One Evangelism.* Wheaton, IL: Victor Books, 1974, 1990.

Elwell, Walter A. *Baker Encyclopedia of the Bible.* Grand Rapids: Baker Book House, 1988.

Falwell, Jonathan. *Innovate Church.* Nashville, TN: B&H Publishing Group, 2008.

Ferguson, Everett. *Church History (Volume One): From Christ to Pre-Reformation.* Grand Rapids: Zondervan, 2005.

Geisler, Norman L, and William E Nix. *A General Introduction to the Bible.* Chicago: Moody Press, 1996.

Geisler, Norman, and David Geisler. *CONVERSATION EVANGELISM: How to Listen and Speak So You Can Be Heard*. Eugene: Harvest House Publishers, 2009.

Graham, F. William. *A Biblical Standard for Evangelists*. Minneapolis, MN: World Wide Publications, 1984.

Greenlee, J Harold. *Introduction to New Testament Textual Criticism*. Peabody: Hendrickson, 1995.

Harris, Robert Laird, Gleason Leonard Archer, and Bruce K Waltke. *Theological Wordbook of the Old Testament*. Chicago: Moody Press, 1999, c1980.

Henrichsen, A. Walter. *Disciples are Made not Born*. Wheaton, Il: Victor Books, 1974.

Hewitt, Gerald Neal. *A Prescription for Healthy Churches: Help for Disintegrating Churches and Directionless Pastors*. Winston-Salem, NC: GNH Publishing, 2001.

Hill, Jonathan. *Zondervan Handbook to the History of Christianity*. Oxford: Lion, 2006.

Hodge, Dean R., David A. Roozen, and eds. *Understanding Church Growth and Decline: 1950-1978*. New York: The Pilgrim Press, 1979.

Hunt, Josh. *Let it Grow*. Grand Rapids: Baker Book House, 1993.

Johnson, W. Ronald. *How Would They Hear if We Do Not Listen?* Nashville: Broadman & Holman Publishers, 1994.

Kennedy, D. James. *Evangelism Explosion*. Wheaton, IL: Tyndale House Publishers, 1977.

Larsen, L. David. *The Evangelism Mandate*. Wheaton: Crossway Books, 1992.

Larue, Gerald. "The Bible as a Political Weapon, Summer 1983, p. 39." *Free Inquiry*, Summer 1983: 36-41.

Little, E. Paul. *How to Give Away Your Faith*. Grand Rapids: Inter-Varsity Press, 1966.

MacArthur, John. *Keys to Spiritual Growth*. Westwood, NJ: Fleming H. Revell Company, 1976, 1991.

Macchia, Stephen A. *Becoming a Healthy Church: 10 Characteristics*. Grand Rapids, MI: Baker Books, 1999.

Mayers, Mark K. *Christianity Confronts Culture: A Strategy for Crosscultural Evangelism*. Grand Rapids : Zondervan, 1987.

McCloskey, Mark. *Tell it Often-Tell it Well*. San Bernardino, CA: Here's Life Publishers, Inc., 1986.

McGavran, Donald A., and Win Arn. *How to Grow a Church: Conversations about Church Growth*. Glendale, CA: Regal Books, 1973.

McRaney, William. *The Art of Personal Evangelism*. Nashville: Broadman & Holman, 2003.

McReynolds, Paul R. *Word Study: Greek-English*. Carol Stream: Tyndale House Publishers, 1999.

Mirriam-Webster, Inc. *Mirriam-Webster's Collegiate Dictionary. Eleventh Edition*. Springfield: Mirriam-Webster, Inc., 2003.

Mitchell, Michael R. *Leading, Teaching, and Making Disciples: World-Class Education in the Church, School, and Home*. Bloomington: Crossbooks, 2010.

Morgenthaler, Sally. *Worship Evangelism*. Grand Rapids: Zondervan Publishing House, 1995.

Mounce, William D. *Mounce's Complete Expository Dictionary of Old & New Testament Words*. Grand Rapids, MI: Zondervan, 2006.

Norman, R. Stanton. *The Baptist Way: Distinctives of a Baptist Church*. Nashville: Broadman & Holman Publishers, 2005.

Oden, Thomas C. *Ministry Through Word and Sacrament, Classic Pastoral Care*. New York: Crossroad, 1989.

Ortberg, John. *The Life You've Always Wanted: Spiritual Disciplines for Ordinary People*. Grand Rapids, MI: Zondervan, 2002.

Packer, J. I. *Evangelism and Sovereignty of God*. Downers Grove, Il: InterVarsity Press, 1961.

Packer, J. I. *Evangelism and the Sovereignty of God*. Downers Grove, IL: InterVarsity Press, 1979.

Peterson, Jim. *Living Proof*. Colorado Springs: Navpress, 1989.

Pickard, Nellie. *What Do You Say When...* Grand Rapids: Baker Book House, 1988.

Pippert, M. Rebecca. *Out of the Saltshaker & Into the World*. Downers Grove, Il: InterVarsity Press, 1979.

Posterski, C. Donald. *Reinventing Evangelism*. Downers Grove, IL: InterVarsity Press, 1989.

Rainer, S. Thomas. *Evangelism in the Twenty-First Century*. Wheaton, IL: Harold Shaw Publishers, 1989.

Rainer, Thomas S. *Effective Evangelistic Churches.* Nashville: Broadman & Holman Publishers, 1996.

Reid, Alvin. *Introduction to Evangelism.* Nashville: Boardman & Holmes , 1998.

Reid, Alvin L. *Radically Unchurched: Who They are and How to Reach Them.* Grand Rapids: Kregel, 2002.

Roberts, Alexander, James Donaldson, and A. Cleveland Coxe. *THE ANTE-NICENE FATHERS 1: The Apostolic Fathers with Justin Martyr and Irenaeus.* Buffalo: The Christian Literature Company, 1885.

Robinson, Darrell W. *Total Church Life: How to be a First Century Chrurch.* Nashville, TN: Briadman and Holman, 1997.

Sisson, Dick. *Evangelism Encounter.* Chicago, IL: Victor Books, 1988.

Stetzer, Ed, and David Putman. *Breaking the Missional Code: Your Church Can Become a Missionary in Your Community.* Nashville: Broadman & Holman, 2006.

Stott, John. *The Art of Preaching in the Twentieth Century: Between Two Worlds.* Grand Rapids, MI: Wm. B. Eerdmans, 1994.

Sutton, Jerry. *A Primer on Biblical Preaching.* Bloomington, IN: CrossBooks, 2011.

Vincent, Marvin. *Word Studies in the New Testament.* Bellingham: Logos Research Systems, 2002.

Vine, W E. *Vine's Expository Dictionary of Old and New Testament Words.* Nashville: Thomas Nelson, 1996.

Westerhoff, John. *Spiritual Life: The Foundation for Preaching and Teaching*. Louisville, KY: Westminister John Knox Press, 1994.

Whitney, Donald S. *Spiritual Disciplines for the Christian Life with Bonus Content (Pilgrimage Growth Guide)*. Colorado Springs, CO: Navpress, 1991.

Wuest, Kenneth S. *Wuest's Word Studies from the Greek New Testament: For the English Reader*. Grand Rapids: Eerdmans, 1997, c1984.

Zodhiates, Spiros. *The Complete Word Study Dictionary: New Testament*. Chattanooga: AMG Publishers, 2000, c1992, c1993.

www.ingramcontent.com/pod-product-compliance
Lightning Source LLC
LaVergne TN
LVHW011346080426
835511LV00005B/148